2000-2001
Edition

Ten-Tronck's™

Celebrity Web Site & E-Mail Directory

2000-2001
Edition

Ten-Tronck's™

Celebrity Web Site & E-Mail Directory

Published by:

 Axiom Information Resources

Ann Arbor, Michigan 48107

Celebrity Web Site & E-Mail Directory™
Published by Axiom Information Resources
Ann Arbor, Michigan 48107 USA

Copyright ©2000 Axiom Information Resources

All rights reserved. No part of this publication
may be reproduced or distributed in any form or
by any means, or stored in a data base or retrieval
system, without the prior written permission of
the publishers.

Published by:
Axiom Information Resources
P.O. Box 8015
Ann Arbor, MI 48107

Printed in USA
ISBN 0-943213-33-9
ISSN 1524-8704

Cover Design by: Concialdi Design

SPECIAL SALES
The Celebrity Web Site & E-Mail Directory™ is
available at special quantity discounts
for bulk purchases. For information write:

Axiom Information Resources
P.O. Box 8015-WEB
Ann Arbor, MI 48107

Contents

                Introduction 1

Section 1   **Movie and TV Stars** 3
                Major Stars of the Movies and Television
                from the 30's through the 90's

Section 2   **Famous Musicians and Recording Stars** 31
                Stars from Classical,
                Pop, Rap, Rock,
                Soul, and Jazz Music

Section 3   **Sports Stars** 69
                Celebrities from Major
                Sports: Baseball, Football, Basketball,
                Golf, Tennis, Olympians,
                Hall of Famers and Executives

Section 4   **Politicians and Royalty** 77
                Congressional Leaders,
                State and Local Politicians,
                Supreme Court Justices,
                White House Executives,
                World Leaders and Royal Families

Section 5   **Other Famous People** 89
                Artists, Authors, Cartoonists,
                Super Models, Famous Businessmen,
                Radio Personalities, Religious
                Figures and Other Celebrated People

Section 6   **E-Mail Addresses** 99

Order Blank and Customer Response Form (See Back Page)

Welcome to the *Celebrity Web Site & E-Mail Directory*. This book will serve as an easy-to-use, one-stop guide to the coolest Web Sites and E-Mail addresses of Movie and TV stars, recording artists, athletes, politicians, and assorted other celebrities.

Researchers, librarians, and fans alike will find this to be an invaluable resource. Web sites provide a wealth of information about your favorite celebrities. If you want filmographies, appearance schedules, or biographical facts about a movie star, their web sites are a good place to look. If you want the latest touring schedule or recording information about your favorite singer or music group, it's probably posted on their web site. Or if you want to chat with other fans or purchase merchandise such as T-shirts or CD's, their web site is your best bet.

This book will also help you to send E-mail messages to celebrities. Although some celebrities do not make their E-mail addresses public, they will often provide alternate ways to contact them at their web sites, so it's always a good idea to check there if you're looking to contact celebrities for whatever reason.

A final note: if you find a celebrity's official web-site or E-mail address that is not listed in this book, please let us know by contacting us at http:www.celebritylocator.com.

Special thanks to Mrs. Betty Thompson and The Ann Arbor District Library.

The Celebrity Web Site & E-Mail Directory's Top Five celebrity Web sites:

1. Michael Jackson: http://www.mjifc.com/

2. Prince Charles: http://www.princeofwales.gov.uk/

3. Tiger Woods: http://www.tigerwoods.com/

4. Madonna: http://www.madonnanet.com/guide/

5. Leonard Nimoy: http://www.nimoy.com/

Movies/TV

To place an advertisement in this space,
call 734-761-4842 or E-mail:
axiominfo@celebritylocator.com

To place an advertisement in this space,
call 734-761-4842 or E-mail:
axiominfo@celebritylocator.com

To place an advertisement in this space,
call 734-761-4842 or E-mail:
axiominfo@celebritylocator.com

If you know a celebrity web site or
e-mail address that should be included
in this book, please e-mail it to us at:
axiominfo@celebritylocator.com

Movies/TV   Celebrity Web Site & E-Mail Directory

A _____ A

Abbott And Costello
http://www.city-net.com/abbottandcostellofc/

Robert Addie
http://members.tripod.com/-Sorne/Robt_Addie/index.html

Ben Affleck
http://benaffleck.com/

Jenny Agutter
http://www.geocities.com/Hollywood/Makeup/6275/JenAgutter.html

Jason Alexander
http://www.celebs.net/JasonAlexander/jahome.html

Chad Allen
http://www.geocities.com/WestHollywood/Heights/8274/

Jonelle Allen
http://www-personal.umich.edu/~jcoles/jaindex.html

Karen Allen
http://www.bestware.net/spreng/kare_a/index.html

Tim Allen
http://www.geocities.com/Hollywood/Set/1067/timpage.htm

Woody Allen
http://www.idt.unit.no./~torp/woody/

Carol Alt
http://www.carolalt.net/

Gillian Anderson
http://gaws.ao.net/

Richard Dean Anderson
http://rda.simplenet.com/

If you find some dead links, please let us know at: http://www.celebritylocator.com/

Movies/TV — Celebrity Web Site & E-Mail Directory

Pamela Anderson-Lee
http://www.pamelaandersonlee.com/

Vanessa Angel
http://www.mca.com/tv/weirdscience/cast/angel.html

Jennifer Aniston
http://al.simplenet.com/aniston/

Gabrielle Anwar
http://journey.simplenet.com/anwar/

Christina Applegate
http://members.aol.com/cmdrz96/applegate/calinks.htm

Adam Arkin
http://www.geocities.com/Hollywood/5093/

Beatrice Arthur
http://www.softcom.net/users/robinson/

Linden Ashby
http://www.mindwell.com/~anubis/alibi/

Jane Asher
http://www.jane-asher.co.uk/

Rowan Atkinson
http://www.dsv.su.se/~mats-bjo/bean/bean.html

B _____ B

Laureen Bacall
http://www.claycrystal.com/RM/LBhome.htm

Kevin Bacon
http://www.geocities.com/~ohmystars/

Scott Bairstow
http://www.henge.com/~swanson/

If you find some dead links, please let us know at: http://www.celebritylocator.com/

Movies/TV   Celebrity Web Site & E-Mail Directory

Alec Baldwin
http://home.sprynet.com/sprynet/gpace/absite.html

Stephen Baldwin
http://www.li.net/~yesnet/Opening_Page/opening_page.htm

Christian Bale
http://www.christianbale.org/

Antonio Banderas
http://www.antoniobanderasfans.com/abmain.htm

Majel Barrett-Roddenberry
http://www.roddenberry.com/

Drew Barrymore
http://www.geocities.com/SunsetStrip/6825/drew_barrymore_page.html

Angela Bassett
http://members.tripod.com/~bholness/angela.html

Michelle Bauer
http://www.picpal.com/picpal/mbauer.html

Mr. Bean
http://www.mrbean.co.uk/

Emmanuelle Beart
http://sunflower.singnet.com.sg/~swying/emmanuelle.html

Robert Beltran
http://home.earthlink.net/~peggyc/index.html

Michael Bergin
http://www.baywatchtv.com/cast/bergin.html

Halle Berry
http://www.geocities.com/Hollywood/Set/1592/Halle.html

Michael Biehn
http://www.tropicalshade.com/michael/

If you find some dead links, please let us know at: http://www.celebritylocator.com/

Movies/TV — Celebrity Web Site & E-Mail Directory

Juliette Binoche
http://www.binoche.com/

Fairuza Blak
http://www.fairuza.com/

Humphrey Bogart
http://www.macconsult.com/bogart/

Ron Bohmer
http://www.ronbohmer.com/

Sarah Brightman
http://www.netcore.com/sarahbrightman/

Charles Bronson
http://www.geocities.com/Hollywood/Set/5040/

Pierce Brosnan
http://www.mcs.net/~klast/www/brosnan.html

Clancy Brown
http://www.unl.edu/uevents/mine/clancy.html

Betty Buckley
http://www.bettybuckley.com/

Sandra Bullock
http://sandra.com/

Mike Burger
http://homeandfamily.com/

Brooke Burns
http://www.baywatchtv.com/cast/burns.html

Steve Burton
http://www.geocities.com/Hollywood/Lot/8416/

C _____ C

Nicolas Cage
http://www.best.com/~toni/index.htm

If you find some dead links, please let us know at: http://www.celebritylocator.com/

Movies/TV Celebrity Web Site & E-Mail Directory

Dean Cain
http://fantasia.simplenet.com/lnc/

Neve Campbell
http://www.nevecampbell.dk/

Drew Carey
http://virtuallot.warnerbros.com/cmp/comedy/cm01.htm

Jim Carrey
http://www.geocities.com/Hollywood/9090/

Kim Cattrall
http://web.ukonline.co.uk/Members/matthew.peake/cattrall.htm

Jackie Chan
http://www.trade.net.hk/clients/jackiechan/
(another Jackie Chan site)
http://www.jcconnection.com/

David Chokachi
http://www.baywatchtv.com/cast/chokachi.html

Terry Ike Clanton
http://www.clantongang.com/oldwest/teryresu.html

Andrew Dice Clay
http://gladstone.uoregon.edu/~bhendric/dice.htm

Kristen Cloke
http://www.kristencloke.com/

George Clooney
http://www.geocities.com/Hollywood/2766/

Jennifer Connelly
http://www.qbc.clic.net/~birdy/jc/

Sean Connery
http://www.mcs.net/~klast/www/connery.html

Billy Connolly
http://www.sarsen.demon.co.uk/billy/billy.html

If you find some dead links, please let us know at: http://www.celebritylocator.com/

Movies/TV Celebrity Web Site & E-Mail Directory

Kevin Costner
http://www.geocities.com/Hollywood/7555/

Courteney Cox
http://www.geocities.com/~constantlycc/

Peter Coyote
http://www.petercoyote.com/

Yvonne Craig
http://yvonnecraig.com/

Russell Crowe
http://www.csh.rit.edu/~halle/russell.html

Macaulay Culkin
http://www.axe.net/culkin/

D   D

Timothy Dalton
http://www.timothydalton.com/

Matt Damon
http://mattdamon.com/

Claire Danes
http://www.tnef.com/claire_danes.html

Rodney Dangerfield
http://www.rodney.com/

Daniel Day-Lewis
http://www.danielday.org/

Derek de Lint
http://www.execpc.com/~pewter/Derek_de_Lint/index.html

Calvert Deforest
http://www.calvertdeforest.com/

If you find some dead links, please let us know at: http://www.celebritylocator.com/

Movies/TV   Celebrity Web Site & E-Mail Directory

Dana Delany
http://www.danadelany.com/index.htm

Michael DeLorenzo
http://members.xoom.com/ladee/

Catherine Deneuve
http://www.generation.net/~vincy/cdeneuve.htm

Cameron Diaz
http://www.cameron-diaz.com/

Leonardo DiCaprio
http://www.leonardodicaprio.com/

Shannen Doherty
http://www.shannen-doherty.simplenet.com

Ami Dolenz
http://www.virtual-designs.com/dolenz/

Robert Downey Jr.
http://www.bserv.com/users/lesliv.htm

David Duchovny
http://www.scibernet.com/xfiles/david/

E   E

Clint Eastwood
http://www.man-with-no-name.com/

Nicole Eggert
http://www.geocities.com/Hollywood/2613/nicole.html

Carmen Electra
http://www.serve.com/carmen/

Jenna Elfman
http://www.microtec.net/~dhouston/

If you find some dead links, please let us know at: http://www.celebritylocator.com/

Movies/TV   Celebrity Web Site & E-Mail Directory

Alison Elliott
http://members.aol.com/Kidkinney/alison.html

Elvira
http://www.elvira.com/

Emilio Estevez
http://www.pacifier.com/~amye/

Rupert Everett
http://www.geocities.com/Athens/Delphi/7724/index.html

F   F

Jeff Fahey
http://www.eskimo.com/~whtrose/fahey.html

Ralph Fiennes
http://members.tripod.com/~ncampos/index.html

Jodie Foster
http://members.tripod.com/~GILREATH/JODIE

Vivica Fox
http://www.vivicafox.com/

Jason David Frank
http://www.geocities.com/Hollywood/9324/jason.html

Mira Furlan
http://mirafurlan.simplenet.com/

G   G

Jennie Garth
http://www.primenet.com/~dpc/jennie/

Sarah Michelle Gellar
http://rc.simplenet.com/smg_page/gallery.html

Mel Gibson
http://www.tropicalshade.com/melgibson/

If you find some dead links, please let us know at: http://www.celebritylocator.com/

Movies/TV   Celebrity Web Site & E-Mail Directory

Whoopi Goldberg
http://www.bestware.net/spreng/whoopi/index.html

Cary Grant
http://www.hep.umn.edu/~jenny/CG_Shrine.html

Hugh Grant
http://users.aol.com/gaelmcgear/hughtimeline.html

Red Green
http://www.redgreen.com/

Bruce Greenwood
http://greenwood.simplenet.com/

Richard Grieco
http://www.rgrieco.com/

H _____ H

Mark Hamill
http://www.geocities.com/Hollywood/Set/4110/

Tom Hanks
http://www.celebsite.com/people/tomhanks/

David Hasselhoff
http://www.baywatchtv.com/cast/hasselhoff.html

Teri Hatcher
http://www.thezone.pair.com/teri/

Salma Hayek
http://www.geocities.com/Hollywood/Studio/1268/

Anne Heche
http://www.celebsite.com/people/anneheche/

David Hedison
http://www.geocities.com/Hollywood/Boulevard/9097/

If you find some dead links, please let us know at: http://www.celebritylocator.com/

Movies/TV   Celebrity Web Site & E-Mail Directory

Lance Henriksen
http://www.rowan.studio.bilp.org/LanceH/lancfilm.htm

Audrey Hepburn
http://www.audreyhepburn.com/

Pee-Wee Herman
http://www.blarg.net/~weazel/peewee.html

Jennifer Love Hewitt
http://allaboutlove.udderinsanity.com/

Dustin Hoffman
http://www.sky.net/~emily/dustin.html

Katie Holmes
http://holmes.starlets.net/

Bob Hope
http://www.bobhope.com/

Sir Anthony Hopkins
http://www.nasser.net/hopkins/

Lisa Howard
http://www.lisahoward.net/

Tom Hulce
http://www.geocities.com/Broadway/3029/hulce.html

Helen Hunt
http://stud2.tuwien.ac.at/~e9525634/

William Hurt
http://www.eonline.com/Facts/People/0,12,47,00.html

I ──────────────────────────────────── I

Michael Ironside
http://www.geocities.com/Hollywood/Hills/3227/

If you find some dead links, please let us know at: http://www.celebritylocator.com/

Movies/TV   Celebrity Web Site & E-Mail Directory

J _____ J

Joshua Jackson
http://www.angelfire.com/mt/pacey/

Samuel L. Jackson
http://member.aol.com/gifhack/main.html

Famke Janssen
http://web.nstar.net/~gkeller/famke/

Don Johnson
http://www.donjohnson.com/

James Earl Jones
http://www.geocities.com/Hollywood/1585/index.html

Shirley Jones
http://www.shirleyjones.com/

Tommy Lee Jones
http://members.aol.com/lukoch2/index.htm

Milla Jovovich
http://www.eskimo.com/~milla/

K _____ K

Mitzi Kapture
http://members.xoom.com/intrinsic/mitzi.htm

Peter Karrie
http://www.peterkarrie.com/

Andy Kaufman
http://andykaufman.jvlnet.com/

Buster Keaton
http://www.netbistro.com/buster/buster.htm

If you find some dead links, please let us know at: http://www.celebritylocator.com/

Movies/TV   Celebrity Web Site & E-Mail Directory

Princess Grace Kelly
http://members.tripod.com/~gracepage/

Nicole Kidman
http://www.vt.edu:10021/G/gmears/kidman/

Val Kilmer
http://www.geocities.com/Hollywood/4532/z11indx.htm

Stan Kirsch
http://www.unl.edu/uevents/mine/stan.html

Kevin Kline
http://people.delphi.com/dramafan/kevinkline.html

Lisa Kudrow
http://www.geocities.com/Hollywood/3142/kudrow.htm

L _____ L

Christopher Lambert
http://www.unl.edu/uevents/mine/christopher.html

Nathan Lane
http://www.nathanlane.com/

A.J. Langer
http://www.geocities.com/TelevisionCity/Studio/1042/

Anthony Lapaglia
http://lapaglia.org

Lucy Lawless
http://www.xenafan.com/

Christopher Lawrence
http://www.geocities.com/Hollywood/Lot/3668/

George Lazenby
http://www.mcs.net/~klast/www/lazenby.html

If you find some dead links, please let us know at: http://www.celebritylocator.com/

Movies/TV   Celebrity Web Site & E-Mail Directory

Bruce Lee
http://www.teleport.com/~danlucas/bruce.html

Jay Leno
http://www.nbc.com/tonightshow/

Laura Linney
http://www.geocities.com/Hollywood/1404/

Heather Locklear
http://www.jimsplace.com/jim/hl.htm

Jennifer Lopez
http://sinema.ihlas.net.tr/Aktor-Aktrisler/JenniferLopez/

Lorna Luft
http://members.aol.com/lornalist/

M   M

Andie MacDowell
http://web.pinknet.cz/AndieMacDowell/

Kyle MacLachlan
http://www.geocities.com/Hollywood/5286/kyle.html

Michael Madsen
http://www.michaelmadsen.com./
(another Michael Madsen site)
http://members.aol.com/madsen1fan/pp22.htm

Julianna Margulies
http://www.fotomayer.de/jules/new/default.htm

Jason Marsden
http://www.phoenix.net/~elissa/jason.htm

James Marshall
http://www.ismi.net/~joemill/

Kellie Martin
http://www.joes.com/home/markrabo/

If you find some dead links, please let us know at: http://www.celebritylocator.com/

Movies/TV   Celebrity Web Site & E-Mail Directory

Steve Martin
http://www.intcity.com/wcguy/

A Martinez
http://www.amartinez.com/

Joseph Mazzello
http://www.he.net/~mike/

Jenny McCarthy
http://www.jenny-mccarthy.com/

Matthew McConaughey
http://www.flash.net/~rana2kay/MattMcPage.html

Dyland McDermott
http://www.capecod.net/~ehahn/dmcdermott/dylan.html

William McNamara
http://www.masscot.com/mcnamara/

Mark Metcalf
http://www.geocities.com/Hollywood/Hills/8018/

Jonathan Rhys Meyers
http://members.tripod.com/~Rhys_Myers/

Dale Midkiff
http://www.geocities.com/TelevisionCity/Studio/1383/

Alyssa Milano
http://www.alyssa.com/

Hayley Mills
http://www.geocities.com/Yosemite/2505/

Marilyn Monroe
http://www.ionet.net/~jellenc/marilyn.html

Elizabeth Montgomery
http://www.bewitched.net/

If you find some dead links, please let us know at: http://www.celebritylocator.com/

Movies/TV Celebrity Web Site & E-Mail Directory

Demi Moore
http://home1.inet.tele.dk/kimbor/demimain.html

Julianne Moore
http://www.julianne-moore.com/

Roger Moore
http://www.mcs.net/~klast/www/moore.html

James Morrison
http://www.mindspring.com/~louisep/jmdg-l/

N _____ N

Liam Neeson
http://www.geocities.com/Hollywood/Set/6510/

Sam Neill
http://sunsite.unc.edu/samneill/

Jack Nicholson
http://home.earthlink.net/~joepez/jack/

Leonard Nimoy
http://www.nimoy.com/

Gena Lee Nolin
http://www.genalee.com/

Kathleen Noone
http://www.allmediapr.com/noone/

Chris North
http://members.aol.com/dwalheim/noth.html

Bill Nye
http://www.nyelabs.com

O _____ O

Renee O'Connor
http://www.impulz.net/~ragnarok/roc.htm

If you find some dead links, please let us know at: http://www.celebritylocator.com/

Movies/TV   Celebrity Web Site & E-Mail Directory

Chris O'Donnell
http://rs2.ch.liv.ac.uk/biry/chris_odonnell.html

Rosie O'Donnell
http://rosieo.warnerbros.com/

David O'Hara
http://www.wardy.org/ohara.html

Maureen O'Hara
http://www.jetcity.com/~beck/mo_title.html

Gary Oldman
http://home.worldonline.nl/~giso/oldman.htm

Larisa Oleynik
http://members.aol.com/GottaLuvLO/

Edward James Olmos
http://xwing.t-one.net/olmos/

Julia Ormond
http://www.vancouver.net/home/cacchioni/julia.htm

P _____ P

Al Pacino
http://members.iquest.net/~jdm/pacino.htm

Kelly Packard
http://www.baywatchtv.com/cast/packard.html

Elaine Paige
http://pages.nyu.edu/~jjb222/elaine/elaine.html

Gwyneth Paltrow
http://www.gwynethpaltrow.org/

Vanessa Paradis
http://welcome.to/vanessa.paradis/

If you find some dead links, please let us know at: http://www.celebritylocator.com/

Movies/TV   Celebrity Web Site & E-Mail Directory

Michael Pare
http://www.MichaelPare.com/

Sarah Jessica Parker
http://www.geocities.com/Hollywood/5159/

Trey Parker
http://www.geocities.com/TelevisionCity/Studio/1751/trey.html

Adrian Paul
http://www.unl.edu/uevents/mine/adrian.html

Ashley Peldon
http://www.allmediapr.com/apeldon/

Courtney Peldon
http://www.allmediapr.com/cpeldon/

Sean Penn
http://www.geocities.com/Hollywood/Bungalow/6339/

Vincent Perez
http://www.jps.net/cris/

Luke Perry
http://www.flash.net/~narnia/luke.htm

Matthew Perry
http://www.geocities.com/Hollywood/3142/perry.htm

Joe Pesci
http://pesci.tierranet.com/joepesci/

Michelle Pfeiffer
http://pfeiffer.arobax.fr/

Bratt Pitt
http://www.thezone.pair.com/celeb/pitt.htm

Natalie Portman
http://www.natalieportman.com/

If you find some dead links, please let us know at: http://www.celebritylocator.com/

Movies/TV   Celebrity Web Site & E-Mail Directory

Chris Potter
http://www.caine.com/cp/

Stephanie Powers
http://members.aol.com/lilreportr/index.html

Freddie Prinze, Jr.
http://www.freddieprinzejr.com/

Q _____ Q

Aidan Quinn
http://www.mindspring.com/~angstgirl/aidan.html

R _____ R

Ingo Rademacher
http://www.ingo.net/

Lexi Randall
http://www.geocities.com/Hollywood/Boulevard/2538/

Keanu Reeves
http://www.keanunet.com/knet.html

Duncan Regehr
http://www.geocities.com/~sjso/
(another Duncan Regehr site)
http://msmoo.simplenet.com/regehr/regehr1.htm

Brad Renfro
http://www.angelfire.com/tn/BradRenfro/

Burt Reynolds
http://www.burtreynolds.com/

Debbie Reynolds
http://www.debbiereynolds.com/

Tim Rice
http://pages.nyu.edu/~jjb222/tim/tr.html

If you find some dead links, please let us know at: http://www.celebritylocator.com/

Movies/TV   Celebrity Web Site & E-Mail Directory

Ariana Richards
http://www.ariana.org/wimg/

Don Rickles
http://www.thehockeypuck.com/

Julia Roberts
http://web.pinknet.cz/~matusek/j_roberts/

Chris Rock
http://members.tripod.com/~Reco_Williams/CHRIS_ROCK.html

Roy Rogers
http://www.royrogers.com/

Will Rogers
http://www.ionet.net:80/~jellenc/rogers.html

Al Roker
http://www.roker.com/

Charlotte Ross
http://charlotteross.simplenet.com/

Tim Roth
http://www.geocities.com/Hollywood/Lot/3753/TimIndex.html

Cynthia Rothrock
http://www.interlog.com/~tigger/rothrock.html

Keri Russell
http://www.sci.fi/~xanthic/keri/

Kurt Russell
http://www.geocities.com/Paris/Bistro/7019/index.html

Kelly Rutherford
http://www.geocities.com/Hollywood/Hills/6813/kelly/index.html

Jeri Lynn Ryan
http://www.jerilynn.com/

If you find some dead links, please let us know at: http://www.celebritylocator.com/

Movies/TV Celebrity Web Site & E-Mail Directory

Meg Ryan
http://members.xoom.com/SSanders/

S _____ S

Antonio Sabato
http://www.geocities.com/Paris/LeftBank/3279/ANTONIO.HTML

Adam Sandler
http://www.adamsandler.com/
(another Adam Sandler site)
http://www.asandler.com/

Susan Sarandon
http://www.chrisbaker.co.uk/

Rob Schneider
http://www.geocities.com/Hollywood/Set/6338/who.html

Arnold Schwarzenegger
http://www.schwarzenegger.com/

David Schwimmer
http://users.aol.com/loraj/dspage.html

Jerry Seinfeld
http://www2.gvsu.edu/%7Emaurerb/Seinfeld.html

Jane Seymour
http://www.janeseymour.org/

Caryn Shalita
http://www.caryn.com/

Brooke Shields
http://www.geocities.com/Hollywood/Hills/2939/

Elisabeth Shue
http://www.elisabeth-shue.com/

Ron Silver
http://members.tripod.com/~Barbara_Robertson/silver.html

If you find some dead links, please let us know at: http://www.celebritylocator.com/

Movies/TV   Celebrity Web Site & E-Mail Directory

Alicia Silverstone
http://www.silverstone.org/

Richards Simmons
http://www.richardsimmons.com/

Gary Sinise
http://www.planetx.com/sinise/

Christian Slater
http://www.magna.com.au/~hodge/cslater.html

Anna Nicole Smith
http://www.annaonline.com/

Taran Smith
http://members.aol.com/cammy1234/cktns.html

Will Smith
http://www.geocities.com/Hollywood/Studio/4866/

Smothers Brothers
http://www.smothersbrothers.com/

Kevin Sorbo
http://msmoo.simplenet.com/sorbo/sorbo4.htm

Mira Sorvino
http://www.stribble.com/ms/

Talisa Soto
http://members.tripod.com/~pandus/TALISASOTO.html

Kevin Spacey
http://www.spacey.com/

Brent Spiner
http://www.asahi-net.or.jp/~ti3y-itu/

Sylvester Stallone
http://pubweb.acns.nwu.edu/~mmp856/slynxs.htm

If you find some dead links, please let us know at: http://www.celebritylocator.com/

Movies/TV   Celebrity Web Site & E-Mail Directory

Jessica Steen
http://www.jessicasteen.com/

Patrick Stewart
http://members.tripod.com/~PatrickStewart/

Sharon Stone
http://www.serve.com/sharon/sharon.htm

Rider Strong
http://www.riderstrong.com/

T _____ T

Elizabeth Taylor
http://users.deltanet.com/users/dstickne/lizt.htm

Tiffani-Amber Theissen
http://www.teleport.com/~georgeba/tat/tatframe.htm

Charlize Theron
http://www.cryptic.org/theron/

Jonathan Taylor Thomas
http://www.cris.com/~mccormik/j&j.htm

Kristin Scott Thomas
http://djuna.simplenet.com/kst/

Tim Thomerson
http://hometown.aol.com/timthomfc/index.htm

Emma Thompson
http://www.tsdesign.com/mulder/emma/index.html

Lea Thompson
http://members.aol.com/eddiedecho/index.html

Courtney Thorne-Smith
http://www.courtneythornesmith.com/

If you find some dead links, please let us know at: http://www.celebritylocator.com/

Movies/TV   Celebrity Web Site & E-Mail Directory

The Three Stooges
http://www.3-stooges.com/

Uma Thurman
http://www.paralysis.com/uma/thurman.html

Marisa Tomei
http://www.noaloha.com/tomei/

John Travolta
http://www.sonic.net/~mfortsch/menu.html

Liv Tyler
http://www.pns.it/livtyler/

U   U

Tracey Ullman
http://www.highwired.com/tullman/

Skeet Ulrich
http://www.skeet.ulrich.com/skeet.html

Robert Urich
http://www.roberturich.com/

V   V

Paul Michael Valley
http://members.aol.com/wedoplays/pmvalley.html

Jean-Claude Van Damme
http://www.geocities.com/Hollywood/Academy/7928/index.html

James Van der Beek
http://members.tripod.com/~jvdb_/

Vince Vaughn
http://www.vincev.com/

If you find some dead links, please let us know at: http://www.celebritylocator.com/

Movies/TV   Celebrity Web Site & E-Mail Directory

Sofia Vergara
http://www.sofiavergara.com/

Asia Vieira
http://www.geocities.com/~dhdenney/asia/index.html

Jenna von Oy
http://www.jennavonoy.com/

W   W

Natasha Gregson Wagner
http://www.best.com/~abacus/ngw/natasha.html

Robert Wagner
http://members.xoom.com/robertwagner/

Christopher Walken
http://http1.brunel.ac.uk/~mapgsat/movies/walken/home.html

Ally Walker
http://members.aol.com/Austin1511/Walker.html

Denzel Washington
http://user.pa.net/~joelong/home.htm

Alberta Watson
http://www.albertawatson.com/

John Wayne
http://home.cdsnet.net/~lwood/wayne/wayne.htm

Sigourney Weaver
http://www.fortunecity.com/lavendar/atkinson/35/index.html

Steven Weber
http://www.geocities.com/Hollywood/Lot/7339/index.htm

Mae West
http://www.sirius.com/~kims/maewest.html

If you find some dead links, please let us know at: http://www.celebritylocator.com/

Movies/TV   Celebrity Web Site & E-Mail Directory

Wil Wheaton
http://members.aol.com/cinnae1/page3.htm

Michelle Williams
http://www.michelle-williams.com/

Robin Williams
http://www.socuda.com/rwilliams/

Vanessa Williams
http://www.geocities.com/SunsetStrip/Studio/2139/

Bruce Willis
http://members.xoom.com/bedguy/index.html

Bridgette Wilson
http://www.bridgette.person.dk/

Peta Wilson
http://members.xoom.com/petawilson/

Oprah Winfrey
http://www.oprah.com

Kate Winslet
http://www.abbagirl.com/kate.html

Alicia Witt
http://tnef.com/alicia_witt.html

Elijah Wood
http://www.elijahwood.com/

Edward Woodward
http://www.conubic.com/eqew/equaliz2.html

Kari Wuhrer
http://www.geocities.com/Hollywood/Hills/1404/nspage.html

Noah Wyle
http://www.btinternet.com/~orlando/wyle.htm

If you find some dead links, please let us know at: http://www.celebritylocator.com/

Movies/TV — Celebrity Web Site & E-Mail Directory

Y

Anita Yuen
http://www.famouswomen.com/anita/anita.htm

Chow Yun-Fat
http://www.geocities.com/Athens/8907/factor.html

Z

Billy Zane
http://www.bluedevil.com/bz/

Renee Zellweger
http://www.townecryernews.com/

Catherine Zeta Jones
http://www.geocities.com/Hollywood/Trailer/5358/

Zima Sisters
http://www.teleport.com/~patv/zimasis.htm

Stephanie Zimbalist
http://jamesbond.simplenet.com/remingtonsteele/zimbalist/

Daphne Zuniga
http://members.aol.com/xzaphodb/page1.htm

If you find some dead links, please let us know at: http://www.celebritylocator.com/

Music

To place an advertisement in this space,
call 734-761-4842 or E-mail:
axiominfo@celebritylocator.com

To place an advertisement in this space,
call 734-761-4842 or E-mail:
axiominfo@celebritylocator.com

To place an advertisement in this space,
call 734-761-4842 or E-mail:
axiominfo@celebritylocator.com

If you know a celebrity web site or
e-mail address that should be included
in this book, please e-mail it to us at:
axiominfo@celebritylocator.com

Music   Celebrity Web Site & E-Mail Directory

A   A

Aaliyah
http://www.angelfire.com/az/megaaaliyahsite/index.html

ABBA
http://www.fi.muni.cz/~hudec/abba/ABBA.shtml

Able Cain
http://www.netads.com/netads/arts/music/marathon/ac/

AC/DC
http://come.to/ACDC.com

Ace of Base
http://www.aceofbase.net/

Bryan Adams
http://www.bryanadams.com/

Aerosmith
http://www.aerosmith.com/

Alice In Chain
http://www.sonymusic.com/artists/AliceInChains/
(another Alice In Chains site)
http://www.geocities.com/Pentagon/8540/aic.html

All Saints
http://www.londonrecords.com/asframe.html

Allman Brothers
http://www.allmanbrothersband.com/
(another Allman Brother site)
http://www.netspace.org/allmans/

Tori Amos
http://www.toriamos.org/

If you find some dead links, please let us know at: http://www.celebritylocator.com/

Music   Celebrity Web Site & E-Mail Directory

Anathema
http://www.blackmetal.com/~mega/Anathema/

Adam Ant
http://www.adam-ant.net/

Leah Andreone
http://www.leahandreone.com/

Fiona Apple
http://mcguigan.javaweb.net/~fiona/

Aqua
http://www.aqua.dk/

Archer/Park
http://www.traveller.com/archpark/

Tina Arena
http://www.starjump.com/tina/

Louis Armstrong
http://www.foppejohnson.com/armstrong/

Monica Arnold
http://members.aol.com/skegee18/index/daleik.htm

The Articles
http://www.thearticles.com/

Chet Atkins
http://www.chetatkins.com/

Atwater-Donnelly
http://members.aol.com/AubreyFolk/

B _____ B

Baby Snufkin
http://www.jibe.com/snufkin/

If you find some dead links, please let us know at: http://www.celebritylocator.com/

Music   Celebrity Web Site & E-Mail Directory

Johann Sebastian Bach
http://www.jsbach.org/

Bad Boy Entertainment
http://www.badboy-ent.com/flash/

Erykah Badu
http://www.kedar.com/kedar20.htm

Barenaked Ladies
http://www.bnl.org/

Cecilia Bartoli
http://www.lochnet.com/client/gs/cb.html

Beastie Boys
http://www.grandroyal.com/BeastieBoys/

The Beatles
http://www.sonic.net/~custom/beat.html

The Beautiful South
http://www.beautiful-south.co.uk/

Beck
http://www.beck-web.com/

Ben Fold Five
http://www.epiccenter.com/EpicCenter/Benfoldsite/index.qry?artistid=274

Pat Benatar
http://www.benatar.com/

Matraca Berg
http://www.matraca.com

Hector Berlioz
http://www.deltanet.com/~ducky/berlioz.htm

Big Country
http://www.bigcountry.co.uk/

If you find some dead links, please let us know at: http://www.celebritylocator.com/

Music   Celebrity Web Site & E-Mail Directory

Big Bad Voodoo Daddy
http://www.coolsvillerecords.com/bbvd/index.htm

Big Head Todd & the Monsters
http://www.bigheadtodd.com/

Bjork
http://www.resoft.inopera.it/musica/bjork.htm

Black Sabbath
http://www.black-sabbath.com/

Clint Black
http://www.clintblackfans.com/

Black Oak Arkansas
http://www.blackoakarkansas.com/main.html

Blink-182
http://www.blink182.com/

Alpha Blondy
http://www.alphablondy.org/

Michael Bolton
http://www.michaelbolton-fanclub.com/

Trace Bonham
http://www.ozemail.com.au/~msafier/TracyBonham/menu.html

Boom Shaka
http://www.boomshaka.com/

David Bowie
http://www.davidbowie.com/

Boy George
http://www-personal.umich.edu/~geena/boygeorge.html

BoyzIIMen
http://fanasylum.com/boyz2men/

If you find some dead links, please let us know at: http://www.celebritylocator.com/

Music   Celebrity Web Site & E-Mail Directory

Boyzone
http://www.boyzone.co.uk/

Delaney Bramlett
http://www.bluesparadise.com/delaney/

Brandy
http://www.foreverbrandy.com/

The Breeders
http://www.noaloha.com/

Brooks & Dunn
http://www.brooks-dunn.com/

Garth Brooks
http://www.planetgarth.com/

Meredith Brooks
http://www.meredithbrooks.com/main.html

James Brown
http://www.unimedia.fr/sf/jamesbrown/

Julie Brown
http://www.best.com/~fbaker/JulieBrown/

Betty Buckley
http://www.bettybuckley.com/

Jeff Buckley
http://www.creednet.com/

Jimmy Buffett
http://www.soasoas.com/

Solomon Burke
http://www.solomonburke.com/

Bush
http://www.bushnet.com/home/

If you find some dead links, please let us know at: http://www.celebritylocator.com/

# Music	Celebrity Web Site & E-Mail Directory

Kate Bush
http://miso.wwa.com/~vickie/artists/kb.html

Butthole Surfers
http://www.buttholesurfers.com/

Buzzy Bones
http://www.relativityrecords.com/relativity/bizzy/index.html

C _____ C

Cake
http://www.cakemusic.com/

Maria Callas
http://www.callas.it/

Camel
http://www.inertron.com/camel/

Candlebox
http://www.candlebox.com/

Canibus
http://www.canibus.com/

Canned Heat
http://www.cannedheatmusic.com/

Freddy Cannon
http://www.freddyboom.com/

Mariah Carey
http://www.mariahcarey-fanclub.com/

Benny Carter
http://www.lpb.com/benny/

Johnny Cash
http://www.johnnycash.com/

If you find some dead links, please let us know at: http://www.celebritylocator.com/

Music   Celebrity Web Site & E-Mail Directory

Tracy Chapman
http://www.geocities.com/SunsetStrip/Palms/9541/

Ray Charles
http://www.raycharles.com/

Charo
http://www.charo.com/

The Chemical Brothers
http://www.astralwerks.com/chemical/

Cher
http://www.inch.com/~harbur/cher/

Cherry Poppin' Daddies
http://www.netsedge.com/daddies/

Chicago
http://www.chirecords.com/

Coal Chamber
http://www.mysti.com/coalchamber/

Eric Clapton
http://www.kiss.uni-lj.si/%7Ek4mf0026/index.html
(another Eric Clapton site)
http://www.slowhand.net/

Leonard Cohen
http://www.serve.com/cpage/LCohen/

Steve Coleman
http://www.m-base.com/

Judy Collins
http://www.judycollins.com/

Shawn Colvin
http://www.meer.net/~shawn/

If you find some dead links, please let us know at: http://www.celebritylocator.com/

Music   Celebrity Web Site & E-Mail Directory

Commander Cody
http://www.globerecords.com/Cody.html

Harry Connick, Jr.
http://www.connick.com/

Larry Coryell
http://stange.simplenet.com/coryell/

Elvis Costello
http://east.isx.com/~schnitzi/ec/

Cowboy Junkies
http://www.geffen.com/cowboyjunkies/links.html

The Cranberries
http://www.cranberries.ie/

Counting Crows
http://www.countingcrows.com/

Crash Test Dummies
http://www.crashtestdummies.com/

Crosby, Stills & Nash
http://www.alpha.nl/CSN/

Christopher Cross
http://www.christophercross.com/

Sheryl Crow
http://www.amrecords.com/artists/sherylcrow/

The Cure
http://www.thecure.com/

Billy Ray Cyrus
http://www.poeticpage.net/linksbrc.html

D   D

Mark Dacascos
http://dacascos.com/

If you find some dead links, please let us know at: http://www.celebritylocator.com/

Music   Celebrity Web Site & E-Mail Directory

Dick Dale
http://www.dickdale.com/

Charlie Daniels
http://www.charliedaniels.com/

Bobby Darin
http://www.geocities.com/Hollywood/Academy/7011/darin.html

Ray Davies
http://www.raydavies.com/

Miles Davis
http://www.milesdavis.com/

DC Talk
http://www.ardent-enthusiast.com/

Dead Man's Curve
http://www.jukebox.demon.co.uk/

Deftones
http://www.deftones.com/

Depeche Mode
http://www.depeche-mode.com/

Rick Derringer
http://www.rickderringer.com/

Al Di Meola
http://www.aldimeola.com/

The Dixie Chicks
http://www.sonymusic.com/labels/nashville/DixieChicks/

Ani Diffranco
http://www.anidifranco.net/

Celine Dion
http://www.celineonline.com/

If you find some dead links, please let us know at: http://www.celebritylocator.com/

Music Celebrity Web Site & E-Mail Directory

Placido Domingo
http://www.placidodomingo.com/

The Doors
http://www.the-doors.com/

Dr. Dre
http://wallofsound.go.com/artists/drdre/home.html

Dru Hill
http://www.geocities.com/SunsetStrip/Palms/7631/druindex.html

Duran Duran
http://www.mindsync.com/tdfn/

Bob Dylan
http://www.bobdylan.com/

E E

Eagle
http://badger.ac.brocku.ca/~bi95aa/sadcafe.html

Earth, Wind & Fire
http://www.earthwindandfire.com/

Madeline Eastman
http://www.madelineeastman.com/

Duke Ellington
http://duke.fuse.net/

Joe Ely
http://www.ely.com/

Enigma
http://www.enigma3.com/

Peter Erskine
http://petererskine.com/

Music   Celebrity Web Site & E-Mail Directory

Gloria Estefan
http://www.epiccenter.com/EpicCenter/custom/56/

Melissa Etheridge
http://www.melissaetheridge.com/

Eve 6
http://www.bugjuice.com/eve6/index.html

F   F

Maynard Ferguson
http://www.xs4all.nl/~maynard/

Ferron
http://ferronweb.com/

First Church Of Chumbawamba
http://www.chumba.com/

Fleetwood Mac
http://www.fleetwoodmac.net/

John Fogerty
http://www.johnfogerty.com/

Frankie Ford
http://www.frankieford.com/

Vivica Fox
http://www.vivicafox.com/

Peter Frampton
http://www.frampton.com/

Aretha Franklin
http://webhome.globalserve.net/ebutler

G   G

Peter Gabriel
http://realworld.on.net/pg/menu.html

If you find some dead links, please let us know at: http://www.celebritylocator.com/

Music   Celebrity Web Site & E-Mail Directory

Garbage
http://www.garbage.com/

Jerry Garcia
http://www.sirius.com/~jmelloy/jlink.html

Genesis
http://www.genesis-web.com/

Vince Gill
http://www.vincegill.com/

Goo Goo Dolls
http://www.wbr.com/GooGooDolls/

Lesley Gore
http://listen.to/lesley

Graham Central Station
http://www.gcsweb.org/

Amy Grant
http://www.amygrant.com/foa/

Grateful Dead
http://www.dead.net/

Dobie Gray
http://www.dobiegray.com/

Green Day
http://www.greenday.net/

Casey Lee Green
http://www.caseyleegreen.com/

Grooverider
http://www.grooverider.com/

The Gumbi Band
http://www.thegumbiband.com/

If you find some dead links, please let us know at: http://www.celebritylocator.com/

Music   Celebrity Web Site & E-Mail Directory

Guns N' Roses
http://www.bzzt.com/gnrbar/

Buddy Guy
http://www.buddyguys.com/

H _____ H

Charlie Haden
http://interjazz.com/haden/

Loretta Hagen
http://members.aol.com/LorettaHag/page1.html

Merle Haggard
http://www.thehag.com/

Hall & Oates
http://iwc.pair.com/hall_oates/

Scott Hamilton
http://members.aol.com/revjoelle/index.html

Hanson
http://hansonline.com/

George Harrison
http://www.paragraph.se/beatles/harrison.html

Deborah Harry
http://www.primenet.com/~lab/DHDeborahHarry.html

PJ Harvey
http://pjh.org/online/

Ronnie Hawkins
http://www.pipcom.com/~thehawk/index.html

Isaac Hayes
http://www.isaachayes.com/

If you find some dead links, please let us know at: http://www.celebritylocator.com/

44

Music Celebrity Web Site & E-Mail Directory

Hepcat
http://nelson.olm.net/Hepcat/hepcat.html

John Hiatt
http://prime-mover.cc.waikato.ac.nz/Hiatt.html

Hieroglyphics
http://www.hieroglyphics.com/

Tish Hinojosa
http://www.wbr.com/tishhinojosa/

Hiroshima
http://www.hiroshimamusic.com/

Hit Me !!
http://www.hitme.net/

Whitney Houston
http://ourworld.compuserve.com/homepages/Exhale_Tonight/

I   I

Ice Cube
http://www.icecube.com/

Iced Earth
http://www.icedearth.com/

Natalie Imbruglia
http://www.imbruglia.com/

Indigo Girls
http://www.epiccenter.com/EpicCenter/IndigoGirls/

Insane Clown Posse
http://www.insaneclownposse.com/

INXS
http://www.inxs.com/inxs/

If you find some dead links, please let us know at: http://www.celebritylocator.com/

Music   Celebrity Web Site & E-Mail Directory

Iron Butterfly
http://www.ironbutterfly.com/

J ──────────────────────────── J

Alan Jackson
http://www.tpoint.net/~wallen/country/alan-jackson.html

Irene Jackson
http://www.islandnet.com/~woloshen/ijackson.html

Janet Jackson
http://www.janet.nu/

Joe Jackson
http://www.jj-archive.net/

Michael Jackson
http://www.mjifc.com/

Jana Jae
http://www.janajae.com/

Tommy James
http://www.tommyjames.com/

Jamiroquai
http://www.jamiroquai.co.uk/jamiroquai/

Jane's Addiction
http://www.janesaddiction.com/

Jars of Clay
http://www.jarsofclay.com/

Jay-Z
http://listen.to/jay-z

Wyclef Jean
http://www.wyclef.com/wyclefindex.html

If you find some dead links, please let us know at: http://www.celebritylocator.com/

Music Celebrity Web Site & E-Mail Directory

Jefferson Airplane
http://grove.ufl.edu/~number6/Jefferson.Airplane/airplane.html

Jesus Lizard
http://hollywoodandvine.com/thejesuslizard/mainpage.shtml

Jewel
http://www.jeweljk.com/main/

Billy Joel
http://www.billyjoel.com/

Elton John
http://ej.kylz.com/

Al Jolson
http://www.jolson.org/

Quincy Jones
http://www.duke.edu/~jcf3/

Journey
http://journey.simplenet.com/

Tom Joyner
http://www.tjms.com/

Ashley Judd
http://twomoons.simplenet.com/thealtar/

K   K

Mike Keneally
http://www.moosenet.com/keneally.html

KerbStar
http://www.krebstar.com/

Chaka Khan
http://www.chakakhan.com/

If you find some dead links, please let us know at: http://www.celebritylocator.com/

Music Celebrity Web Site & E-Mail Directory

Rabih El-Khawli
http://home.echo-on.net/~rkawli/rabihf.html

Angelique Kidjo
http://wwwusers.imaginet.fr/~kidjo/

Kill Creek
http://www.killcreek.com/

B.B. King
http://www.worldblues.com/bbking/

The King's Singers
http://www.singers.com/kings.html

The Kinks
http://kinks.it.rit.edu/

Kiss
http://KissAsylum.com

KMFDM
http://www.kmfdm.net/

David Knopfler
http://www.knopfler.com/

Korn
http://www.korn.com/

Lenny Kravitz
http://www.virginrecords.com/kravitz/index4.html

Krs-One
http://www.peeps.com/krs-one/

Ruriko Kuboh
http://www.sentex.net/~sardine/ruriko.html

Ed Kuepper
http://server.tt.net/hot/kuepper/

If you find some dead links, please let us know at: http://www.celebritylocator.com/

Music   Celebrity Web Site & E-Mail Directory

L   L

Ladysmith Black Mambazo
http://www.mambazo.com/

Greg Lake
http://www.dynrec.com/lake/lake.html

David Lanz
http://www.davidlanz.com/

Terry Larch
http://members.tripod.com/~larch/index.html

Led Zeppelin
http://www.led-zeppelin.com/

Sonny Boy Lee
http://www.sonnyboylee.com/

Richard Leech
http://www.richardleech.com/

Legendary Pink Dots
http://www.brainwashed.com/lpd/

Danni Leigh
http://www.dannileigh.com/

John Lennon
http://www.paragraph.se/beatles/lennon.html

Julian Lennon
http://www.geocities.com/Hollywood/Boulevard/2801/index.html

Brad Little
http://www.bradlittle.com/

Loverboy
http://www.geocities.com/SunsetStrip/Frontrow/3650

If you find some dead links, please let us know at: http://www.celebritylocator.com/

Music   Celebrity Web Site & E-Mail Directory

Mark Lowry
http://www.marklowry.com/

Lucky Dude
http://www.luckydube.com/

Lynyrd Skynyrd
http://www.skynyrd.com/ring.html

M _____ M

Rita MacNeil
http://www.ritamacneil.com/

Madness
http://www.madness.co.uk/

Madonna
http://www.madonnanet.com/guide/

Malaika
http://www.malaika.ca/

Man...or Astro-man?
http://www.astroman.com/

Manhattan Brass Quintet
http://www.quicklink.com/~antman/MBQ/

Manic Street Preachers
http://www.manics.co.uk/

Barry Manilow
http://www.netfusion.com/maniweb/

Andrea Marcovicci
http://www.galender.com/andrea/

Marcy Playground
http://www.marcyplayground.com/

If you find some dead links, please let us know at: http://www.celebritylocator.com/

Music Celebrity Web Site & E-Mail Directory

Kitty Margolis
http://www.kittymargolis.com/

Marillion
http://www.marillion.com/

Marilyn Manson
http://www.marilynmanson.net/

Marky Mark
http://www.markymark.com/

Bob Marley
http://www.niceup.com/marley.html

Ziggy Marley
http://www.cnotes.com/cnotes.artists/ziggy.html

Richard Marx
http://www.richardmarx.com/

Dana Mase
http://www.danamase.com/

Massive Attack
http://the-raft.com/massive/index.html

MasterP
http://masterp.org/

Matchbox 20
http://www.geocities.com/SunsetStrip/Backstage/1135/

Dave Matthews Band
http://www.dmband.com/

Max Creek
http://www.maxcreek.com/

Martina McBride
http://www.martina-mcbride.com/

If you find some dead links, please let us know at: http://www.celebritylocator.com/

Music — Celebrity Web Site & E-Mail Directory

Paul McCartney
http://www.mplcommunications.com/mccartney/

Mindy McCready
http://www.mindymccready.com/

Reba McEntire
http://www.reba.com/

Bobby McFerrin
http://www.bobbymcferrin.com/home.html

Tim McGraw
http://www.funzone4mcgraw.com/

Sarah McLachlan
http://www.sarahmclachlan.com/

Mighty Sam Mclain
http://www.mightysam.com/

Meat Loaf
http://www.1webplaza.com/meatloaf.html

Medeski, Martin & Wood
http://www.mmw.net/

John Mellencamp
http://www.mellencamp.com/

Melon Patch
http://www.melonpatch.com/melon/

Men out Loud
http://www.menoutloud.com/

Natalie Merchant
http://www.brsite.com/10kmaniacs/nams119.htm

Freddie Mercury
http://www.webring.org/cgi-bin/webring?ring=freddiering&list

If you find some dead links, please let us know at: http://www.celebritylocator.com/

Music Celebrity Web Site & E-Mail Directory

Metallica
http://www.metclub.com/

Pat Metheny
http://www.ecmrecords.com/ecm/artists/535.html

Method Man
http://www.defjam.com/artists/method/method.html

George Michael
http://www.ozemail.com.au/~alhatu/gm.htm

Bette Midler
http://www.nwrain.net/~jstewart/bettehome.htm

Mighty Mighty Bosstones
http://www.geocities.com/SunsetStrip/Towers/6931/

Charles Mingus
http://www.mingusmingusmingus.com/

Liza Minnelli
http://www.oberlin.edu/~dfortune/lizaonline.html

Dannii Minoque
http://www.dannii.com/

Miss Elliott
http://www.missy-elliott.com/

Joni Mitchell
http://www.jonimitchell.com/

Moby
http://www.moby.org/

Moby Grape
http://www.geocities.com/SunsetStrip/1256/

Katy Moffatt
http://members.aol.com/klmoffatt/index.html

If you find some dead links, please let us know at: http://www.celebritylocator.com/

Music   Celebrity Web Site & E-Mail Directory

T.S. Monk
http://www.jazzcorner.com/monk.html

The Monkees
http://www.monkees.net/

Moody Blues
http://www.moodyblues.co.uk/

Lorrie Morgan
http://www.Lorrie.com

Alanis Morissette
http://www.alanismorissette.net/

Morphine
http://www.rykodisc.com/RykoInternal/Features/121/default.htm

Van Morrison
http://corsica.ucs.sfu.ca/~hayward/van/

Motley Crue
http://www.motley.com/

Mott the Hoople
http://public.logica.com/~perkinsa/hunter-mott/

Mudhoney
http://www.unofficial-mudhoney.com/

David Lee Murphy
http://www.countryhome.simplenet.com/dlm1.html

Charles Musselwhite
http://www.rosebudus.com/musselwhite/

N _____ N

N' Sync
http://www.nsync.com/

Music   Celebrity Web Site & E-Mail Directory

David Nelson Band
http://www.nelsonband.com/

Michael Nesmith
http://198.49.210.81/nesmith.asp

New Kids On The Block
http://www.nkotb.com/ontheweb/bffer/

New Order
http://www.interlog.com/~james/NewOrder/

Wayne Newton
http://www.geocities.com/SunsetStrip/Palms/8994/

Olivia Newton-John
http://www.onlyolivia.com/onj.html

Nirvana
http://pw1.netcom.com/~dperle/nirvana/nirvlinks.html

Nitty Gritty Dirt Band
http://www.nittygritty.com/

No Doubt
http://www.nodoubt.com/

NOFX
http://www.crackedass.com/nofx/

Notorious B.I.G.
http://www.geocities.com/NapaValley/4035/big.html

Ted Nugent
http://TheWild.Nuge.Com/JNGonzo/nuge.html

Steve Nystrup
http://www.xenonarts.com/music/nystrup/index.html

If you find some dead links, please let us know at: http://www.celebritylocator.com/

Music   **Celebrity Web Site & E-Mail Directory**

O   O

Oak Ridge Boys
http://www.oakridgeboys.com/

Oasis
http://www.oasisinet.com/

Ocean Colour Scene
http://www.oceancolourscene.com/

Sinead O'Connor
http://www.sinead-oconnor.com/

Rosie O'Donnell
http://rosieo.warnerbros.com/

Offspring
http://www.offspring.com/menu.cgi

Oingo Boingo
http://www.oingoboingo.com/

Mike Oldfield
http://tubular.net/

Omar & The Howlers
http://ourworld.compuserve.com/homepages/dr_feelgood_info_service/omar.htm

Once Hush
http://www.oncehush.com/

The Orb
http://www.theorb.com/

Orbital
http://wkweb1.cableinet.co.uk/BaDmUtHa/

Joan Osborne
http://users.aol.com/drldeboer2/htm/jo.htm

If you find some dead links, please let us know at: http://www.celebritylocator.com/

Music   Celebrity Web Site & E-Mail Directory

Ozzy Osbourne
http://www.ozzynet.com/

The Osmonds
http://www.osmond.com/

The Outhere Brothers
http://www.masscot.com/aureus/outhere.html

P _____ P

Pantera
http://www.wco.com/~pantera/

Jon Kimura Parker
http://www.kimura.com/

Gram Parsons
http://www.gramparsons.com/gramhome.html

Dolly Parton
http://www.bestware.net/spreng/dolly/index.html

Luciano Pavarotti
http://www.lucianopavarotti.it/

Pavement
http://www.slip.net/~pavement/

Pearl Jam
http://www.fivehorizons.com/

Pessimist Black Death Metal
http://www.sting-ray.com/pessimist/

Michael Peterson
http://www.michaelpeterson.com/

Pet Shop Boys
http://www.xs4all.nl/~pwb/psb/

If you find some dead links, please let us know at: http://www.celebritylocator.com/

Music Celebrity Web Site & E-Mail Directory

Tom Petty
http://www-personal.interkan.net/~tomrat/Tom_Petty.html

Liz Phair
http://members.aol.com/guyville/

Phish
http://www.phish.com/

Pink Floyd
http://www.jdfdesign.com/floyd/welcome.html

Pixies
http://www.ozemail.com.au/~thrashin/pixies.htm

The Platters
http://www.imall.com/stores/platters/

Poi Dog Pondering
http://www.rocknroll.net/poi/

Point of Grace
http://www.wordrecords.com/pog/

Jean-Luc Ponty
http://www.ponty.com/

Iggy Pop
http://www.kweb.it/iggy/

Portishead
http://www.portishead.co.uk/

Elvis Presley
http://www.elvis-presley.com/

Gary Primich
http://members.aol.com/gprimich/welcome.htm

Primus
http://www.primussucks.com/

If you find some dead links, please let us know at: http://www.celebritylocator.com/

Music — Celebrity Web Site & E-Mail Directory

Prince (formely known)
http://www.love4oneanother.com/

Prodigy
http://www.prodigy.co.uk/

Psychobilly
http://www.wreckingpit.com/

Giacomo Puccini
http://www.puccini.it/

Puff Daddy
http://www.badboy-ent.com/flash/

Pulp
http://www.rise.co.uk/pulp/

Q ———————————————————— Q

Queen
http://queen-fip.com/

Queensryche
http://www.queensryche.com/

R ———————————————————— R

Radiohead
http://radiohead.zoonation.com/

Rage Against The Machine
http://www.ratm.com/

Bonnie Raitt
http://home.worldonline.nl/~dalmeier/bonnie.htm

Rammstein
http://www.rammstein.com/

If you find some dead links, please let us know at: http://www.celebritylocator.com/

Music   Celebrity Web Site & E-Mail Directory

The Ramones
http://www.kauhajoki.fi/~jplaitio/ramones.html

Rancid
http://www.nyct.net/~damaged/rancid.html

Collin Raye
http://collin-raye.com/

Red Hot Chili Peppers
http://www.redhotchilipeppers.net/

Red House Painters
http://www.kdesigns.com/rhp/

Lou Reed
http://www.loureed.org/

Cliff Richard
http://www.starnet.com.au/sheppard/2cliff.html

LeAnn Rimes
http://www.rimestimes.com/

Majel Roddenberry
http://www.roddenberry.com/

Tommy Roe
http://www.tommyroe.com/

Rolling Stones
http://www.angelfire.com/pa/redlands/links.html

RUSH
http://www.r-u-s-h.com/

Tom Rush
http://www.tomrush.com/

Jeri Lynn Ryan
http://www.jerilynn.com/

If you find some dead links, please let us know at: http://www.celebritylocator.com/

Music   Celebrity Web Site & E-Mail Directory

S   S

Melanie Safka
http://ourworld.compuserve.com/homepages/David_Boldinger/melanie.htm

Buffy Saint-Marie
http://hookomo.aloha.net/~bsm/

Lea Salonga
http://www.columbia.edu/~jc309/lea/

Carlos Santana
http://www.santana.com/

Joe Satriani
http://www.satriani.com/

Savage Garden
http://www.savagegarden.com/main.html

Savatage
http://www.savatage.com/

Seal
http://www.wbr.com/seal/index.html

Brady Seals
http://bradyseals.com/

Sebadoh
http://www.subpop.com/bands/sebadoh/website/

See Jane Run
http://www.seejanerun.com/

Bob Seger
http://www.execpc.com/~pblock/seger.html

Sepultura
http://www.roadrun.com/artists/sepultura/homepage.htm

If you find some dead links, please let us know at: http://www.celebritylocator.com/

Music　　　Celebrity Web Site & E-Mail Directory

Sex Pistols
http://www.virginrecords.com/sex_pistols/

Sha Na Na
http://www.shanana.com/

Tupac Shakur
http://tupac.net/top40/index.html
(another Tupac Shakur site)
http://hem.passagen.se/deathrow/index.htm

Kevin Sharp
http://www.kevinsharp.com/

Vonda Shepard
http://www.vesperalley.com/

Silverchair
http://www.chairpage.com/

Frank Sinatra
http://www.sinatralist.com/

Roni Size
http://www.polygram-us.com/mondo/roni_size/story.html

Sly & Family Stone
http://www.slyfamstone.com/

Smashing Pumpkins
http://www.netphoria.org/

Patti Smith
http://www.phtp.com/

Snoop Doggy Dogg
http://www.snoopdogg.com/

Son Volt
http://www.wbr.com/SonVolt/

If you find some dead links, please let us know at: http://www.celebritylocator.com/

Music

Celebrity Web Site & E-Mail Directory

Soundgarden
http://www.imusic.com/soundgarden/

John Philip Sousa
http://plato.digiweb.com/~dlovrien/sousa/

Britney Spears
http://surf.to/britneyspears

Spice Girls
http://www.angelfire.com/ny/spicelinks/index.html

Spinal Tap
http://www.spinaltap.com/

Bruce Springsteen
http://www.kfunigraz.ac.at/astwww/mst/bruce_noframes.html

Squirrel Nut Zippers
http://www.snzippers.com/

Lisa Stahl
http://www.geocities.com/Hollywood/Studio/9126/

Ringo Starr
http://www.paragraph.se/beatles/ringo.html

Steely Dan
http://www.steelydan.com/

Rod Stewart
http://www.rodstewartlive.com/

Ray Stevens
http://www.raystevens.com/

Sting
http://www.slac.com:80/u/blakaddr/sting/gallery/pic.html

Gale Storm
http://members.xoom.com/ajrfman/GaleStorm2.html

If you find some dead links, please let us know at: http://www.celebritylocator.com/

Music   Celebrity Web Site & E-Mail Directory

George Strait
http://www.georgestrait.com/flashindex.htm

Barbra Streisand
http://members.aol.com/barbramusc/index.html

Marty Stuart
http://www.designer.com/martystuart

Sub Pop Bands
http://www.subpop.com/bands/bhappening/bhappening.html

Suede
http://www.thelondonsuede.com/

Andy Summers
http://www.andysummers.com/

T   T

Talking Heads
http://www.talking-heads.net/

Kem Tamplin
http://www.kentamplin.com/

James Taylor
http://www.james-taylor.com/

Teenage Fanclub
http://www.teenagefanclub.com/

The Tenison Twins
http://www.tenisontwins.com/

John Tesh
http://www.tesh.com/

They Might Be Giants
http://www.tmbg.com/

If you find some dead links, please let us know at: http://www.celebritylocator.com/

Music   Celebrity Web Site & E-Mail Directory

Third Eye Blind
http://www.thirdeyeblind.net/

Tiffany
http://www.tiffany.org/

TLC
http://www.Geocities.com/Hollywood/2320/

Peter Tork
http://wanda.pond.com/%7Ezanapd/tork/

Toto
http://www.toto99.com/

Randy Travis
http://www.randy-travis.com/

Travis Tritt
http://www.travis-tritt.com/

Marshall Tucker Band
http://www.marshalltucker.com/

Tina Turner
http://www.Tina-Turner.com/

Shania Twain
http://www.shania.com/

U   U

U2
http://zoonation.com/indexB.html

Ulali
http://www.ulali.com/

Usher
http://www.usherfanclub.com/

If you find some dead links, please let us know at: http://www.celebritylocator.com/

Music   Celebrity Web Site & E-Mail Directory

V

Steve Vaile
http://www.teleport.com/~gemstone/

Steve Ray Vaughan
http://www.srvfanclub.com/

Suzanne Vega
http://www.vega.net/

Velvet Chain
http://www.lama.com/velvetchain/

Vigilantes of Love
http://www.coaster.com/VOL/

Violent Femmes
http://www.vfemmes.com/

W

Fates Warning
http://www.fateswarning.com/

Wet Willie
http://www.ktb.net/~insync/wet_willie.html

Ian Whitcomb
http://www.picklehead.com/ian.html

Whitesnake
http://members.xoom.com/Whitesnake/

Robin & Linda Williams
http://netsite.dn.net/williams/

Sonny Boy Williams II
http://www.sonnyboy.com/

If you find some dead links, please let us know at: http://www.celebritylocator.com/

Music   Celebrity Web Site & E-Mail Directory

Nancy Wilson (Heart)
http://www.annandnancy.com/

Johnny Winter
http://members.tripod.com/~Plaza_Mike/links.html

Steve Winwood
http://www.stevewinwood.com/

Chely Wright
http://www.chely.com/

X   X

Xuxa
http://www.xuxa.com.br/

Y   Y

Weird Al Yankovic
http://www.weirdal.com/

Yanni
http://www.virginrecords.com/yanni/html/index2.html

Trisha Yearwood
http://www.totallytrisha.com/

Yes
http://www.yesmag.com/

Yothu Yindi
http://www.yothuyindi.com/

Dwight Yoakam
http://www.tpoint.net/~wallen/country/dwight-yoakam.html

Young Dubliners
http://www.youngdubs.com/new.html

If you find some dead links, please let us know at: http://www.celebritylocator.com/

Music   Celebrity Web Site & E-Mail Directory

The Young Gods
http://www.theyounggods.com/

Neil Young
http://www.hyperrust.org/

Z   Z

Frank Zappa
http://www.zappa.com/

ZZ Top
http://www.zztop.com/

If you find some dead links, please let us know at: http://www.celebritylocator.com/

Sports

Sports   Celebrity Web Site & E-Mail Directory

A

Hank Aaron
http://www.cwws.net/~schubert/arn.htm

Helen Alfredsson
http://www.algonet.se/~gulthus/helen/index.htm

B

Oksana Baiul
http://www.superstars.com/oksanabaiul/

Shae-Lynn Bourne
http://www.skate.org/b+k/

Isabelle Brasseur
http://www.skate.org/b+e/

Kurt Browning
http://www.skate.org/browning/

Mark Brunell
http://www.mark-brunell.com/

C

Michael Chang
http://www.mchang.com/

Josee Chouinard
http://www.lehigh.edu/~dg04/josee.shtml

Ben Crenshaw
http://www.bencrenshaw.com/

D

John Daly
http://www.gripitandripit.com/

If you find some dead links, please let us know at: http://www.celebritylocator.com/

Sports Celebrity Web Site & E-Mail Directory

E

Lloyd Eisler
http://www.skate.org/b+e/

F

Melissa Ferrick
http://www.best.com/~kluce/mf.htm

Raymond Floyd
http://www.rayfloyd.com/

G

Ekaterina Gordeeva
http://www.fred.net/paula/katia.html

Sergei Grinkov
http://www.fred.net/paula/grinkov.html

H

Scott Hamilton
http://members.aol.com/revjoelle/index.html

Anita Hartshorn
http://www.fred.net/paula/hart.html

Grant Hill
http://www.inficad.com/~treyman7/index.html

Christine Hough
http://www.skate.org/h+l/

J

Michael Jordan
http://jordan.sportsline.com/

If you find some dead links, please let us know at: http://www.celebritylocator.com/

Sports   Celebrity Web Site & E-Mail Directory

K ──────────────────────────── K

Petri Kokko
http://www.fred.net/paula/rkmain.html

Anna Kournikova
http://www.annak.com/

Victor Kraatz
http://www.skate.org/b+k/

Michelle Kwan
http://www.geocities.com/Vienna/Strasse/3713/

L ──────────────────────────── L

Doug Ladret
http://www.skate.org/h+l/

Tara Lipinski
http://www.taralipinski.com/

Chen Lu
http://www.skate.org/chen/

M ──────────────────────────── M

Elizabeth Manley
http://www.skate.org/manley/

Diego Armando Maradona
http://www.diegomaradona.com

Paul Martini
http://www.skate.org/u+m/

Don Mattingly
http://www.don-mattingly.com/

Michelle McGann
http://www.geocities.com/Wellesley/2526/

If you find some dead links, please let us know at: http://www.celebritylocator.com/

Sports   Celebrity Web Site & E-Mail Directory

Willie McGee
http://www.williemcgee.com/

Mark McGwire
http://www.mcgwire.com/

Phil Mickelson
http://www.phil-mickelson.com/main.nsf

Joe Montana
http://www.joemontanafanclub.com/

N _____ N

Greg Norman
http://www.golfonline.com/greatwhiteshark/index.html

O _____ O

Shaquille O'Neal
http://www.shaq.com/

Brian Orser
http://www.skate.org/orser/

P _____ P

Satchel Paige
http://www.cmgww.com/baseball/paige/paige.html

Gary Payton
http://www.inficad.com/~treyman7/payton2.html

R _____ R

Susanna Rahkamo
http://www.fred.net/paula/rkmain.html

Jerry Rice
http://www.jerryrice.net/

If you find some dead links, please let us know at: http://www.celebritylocator.com/

Sports Celebrity Web Site & E-Mail Directory

David Robinson
http://www.theadmiral.com/

Dennis Rodman
http://lonestar.texas.net/~pmagal/

Pete Rose
http://www.peterose.com/

Babe Ruth
http://www.baberuthmuseum.com/

S   S

Jozef Sabovcik
http://www3.islandnet.com/~luree/joe/jozef.html

Pete Sampras
http://ww1.sportsline.com/u/sampras/

Monica Seles
http://www.ns.net/~victorg/seles/seles.html

Daniel Shank
http://www.ismi.net/~joemill/shank.htm

Elvis Stojko
http://www.skate.org/stojko/

Ozzie Smith
http://www.ozziesmith.com/

Frank Sweiding
http://www.fred.net/paula/hart.html

U   U

Barbara Underhill
http://www.skate.org/u+m/

If you find some dead links, please let us know at: http://www.celebritylocator.com/

Sports   Celebrity Web Site & E-Mail Directory

V

Mo Vaughn
http://www.geocities.com/Colosseum/Track/4242/

Sydne Vogel
http://alaska.simplenet.com/sydne_vogel.html

W

Ted Williams
http://www.hitter.com/

Tiger Woods
http://www.tigerwoods.com/

Paul Wylie
http://www.geocities.com/Colosseum/Arena/1736/

Y

Kristi Yamaguchi
http://www.skate.org/yamaguchi/

Carl Yastrzemski
http://home.epix.net/~brett/yaz.html

If you find some dead links, please let us know at: http://www.celebritylocator.com/

Politics

To place an advertisement in this space,
call 734-761-4842 or E-mail:
axiominfo@celebritylocator.com

To place an advertisement in this space,
call 734-761-4842 or E-mail:
axiominfo@celebritylocator.com

To place an advertisement in this space,
call 734-761-4842 or E-mail:
axiominfo@celebritylocator.com

If you know a celebrity web site or
e-mail address that should be included
in this book, please e-mail it to us at:
axiominfo@celebritylocator.com

Politics — Celebrity Web Site & E-Mail Directory

A

Sec. Medeleine Albright
http://secretary.state.gov/index.html

Rep. Bill Archer (TX)
http://www.house.gov/archer/

Rep. Dick Armey (TX)
http://armey.house.gov/

B

Sec. Bruce Babbitt
http://www.doi.gov/secretary/index.html

Sen. Evan Bayh
http://www.senate.gov/~bayh/

Sen. Joseph A. Biden (DL)
http://www.senate.gov/~biden/

P.M. Tony Blair
http://www.number-10.gov.uk/index.html

Rep. David Bonior (MI)
http://davidbonior.house.gov/

Rep. Mary Bono (CA)
http://www.house.gov/bono/

Sen. Barbara Boxer
http://www.senate.gov/~boxer/

Sen. John Breaux (LA)
http://www.senate.gov/~breaux/

Rep. George Brown (CA)
http://www.house.gov/georgebrown/

If you find some dead links, please let us know at: http://www.celebritylocator.com/

Politics   Celebrity Web Site & E-Mail Directory

Sen. Richard Bryan (NV)
http://www.senate.gov/~bryan/

Sen. Jim Bunning (KY)
http://www.senate.gov/~bunning/

Sen. Conrad Burns (MT)
http://www.senate.gov/~burns/

Gov. George Bush, Jr. (TX)
http://www.governor.state.tx.us/

Gov. Jed Bush (FL)
http://www.state.fl.us/eog/

Sen. Robert Byrd (WA)
http://www.senate.gov/~byrd/

C   C

Sen. Ben Campbell (CO)
http://www.senate.gov/~campbell/

Gov. Paul Cellucci (MA)
http://www.state.ma.us/gov/gov.htm

Sen. John Chafee (FL)
http://www.senate.gov/~chafee/

Prince Charles
http://www.princeofwales.gov.uk/

President Bill Clinton
http://www.whitehouse.gov/WH/EOP/OP/html/OP_Home.html

Hillary Rodhan-Clinton
http://www.whitehouse.gov/WH/EOP/First_Lady/html/HILLARY_Home.html

Sen. Thad Cochran (MS)
http://www.senate.gov/~cochran/

If you find some dead links, please let us know at: http://www.celebritylocator.com/

Politics Celebrity Web Site & E-Mail Directory

William S. Cohen
http://www.defenselink.mil/pubs/almanac/osd.html

Sen. Kent Conrad (ND)
http://www.senate.gov/~conrad/

Rep. John Conyers (MI)
http://www.house.gov/conyers/

Sen. Paul Coverdell (GA)
http://www.senate.gov/~coverdell/

Sen. Larry Craig (ID)
http://www.senate.gov/~craig/

Rep. Phillip Crane (IL)
http://www.house.gov/crane/

Andrew Cuomo
http://www.hud.gov/

D   D

William Daley
http://www.osec.doc.gov/

Sen. Tom Daschle (SD)
http://www.senate.gov/~daschle/

Gov. Gary Davis (CA)
http://www.state.ca.us/s/

Sen. Mike DeWine (OH)
http://www.senate.gov/~dewine/

Princess Diana
http://www.royalnetwork.com/willville/

Rep. John D. Dingell (MI)
http://www.house.gov/dingell/

If you find some dead links, please let us know at: http://www.celebritylocator.com/

Politics   Celebrity Web Site & E-Mail Directory

Sen. Christopher Dobb (CT)
http://www.senate.gov/~dodd/

Sen. Pete Domenici (NM)
http://www.senate.gov/~domenici/

E   E

Queen Elizabeth II
http://www.royal.gov.uk/

Gov. John Engler (MI)
http://www.migov.state.mi.us/migov.html

F   F

Sen. Russell Feingold (WI)
http://www.senate.gov/~feingold/

Sen. Dianne Feinstein (CA)
http://www.senate.gov/~feinstein/

Rep. Barney Frank (MA)
http://www.house.gov/frank/

Louis J. Freeh
http://www.fbi.gov/

G   G

Rep. Richard Gephardt (MO)
http://www.house.gov/gephardt/

Dan Glickman
http://www.usda.gov/agencies/gallery/glickman.htm

V.P. Albert Gore
http://www.whitehouse.gov/WH/EOP/OVP/html/GORE_Home.html

Tipper Gore
http://www.whitehouse.gov/WH/EOP/VP_Wife/index.html

If you find some dead links, please let us know at: http://www.celebritylocator.com/

Politics   Celebrity Web Site & E-Mail Directory

Sen. Slade Gorton (WA)
http://www.senate.gov/~gorton/

Sen. Bob Graham (FL)
http://www.senate.gov/~graham/

Sen. Phil Gramm (TX)
http://www.senate.gov/~gramm/

Sen. Charles Grassley (IA)
http://www.senate.gov/~grassley/

Alan Greenspan
http://www.bog.frb.fed.us/bios/Greenspan.htm

Sen. Judd Gregg (NH)
http://www.senate.gov/~gregg/

H   H

Sen. Chuck Hagert (NE)
http://www.senate.gov/~hagel/

Sen. Tom Harkin (IA)
http://www.senate.gov/~harkin/

Rep. Alcee L. Hastings (FL)
http://www.house.gov/alceehastings/

Sen. Orrin G. Hatch (UT)
http://www.senate.gov/~hatch/

Sen. Jesse Helms (NC)
http://www.senate.gov/~helms/

Alexis M. Herman
http://www.dol.gov/dol/opa/public/sec/secbio.htm

Sen. Fritz Hollings (SC)
http://www.senate.gov/~hollings/

If you find some dead links, please let us know at: http://www.celebritylocator.com/

Politics   Celebrity Web Site & E-Mail Directory

Sen. Kay Bailey Hutchison (TX)
http://www.senate.gov/~hutchison/

Rep. Henry Hyde (IL)
http://www.house.gov/hyde/

Rep. Asa Hutchins (AR)
http://www.house.gov/hutchinson/

J   J

Sen. Tim Jeffords (VT)
http://www.senate.gov/~jeffords/

Sen. Tim Johnson (SD)
http://www.senate.gov/~johnson/

K   K

Anthony Kennedy
http://www.bowdoin.edu/~sbodurt2/court/kennedy.html

Sen. Edward Kennedy (MA)
http://www.senate.gov/~kennedy/

Rep. Patrick Kennedy (RI)
http://www.house.gov/patrickkennedy/

Sen. Robert Kerrey (NE)
http://www.senate.gov/~kerrey/

Sen. John Kerry (MA)
http://www.senate.gov/~kerry/

Sen. Jon Kyl (AZ)
http://www.senate.gov/~kyl/

L   L

Sen. Mary Landrieu (LA)
http://www.senate.gov/~landrieu/

If you find some dead links, please let us know at: http://www.celebritylocator.com/

Politics — Celebrity Web Site & E-Mail Directory

Rep. Tom Lantos (CA)
http://www.house.gov/lantos/

Rep. Steve Largent (OK)
http://www.house.gov/largent/

Sen. Frank Lautenberg (NJ)
http://www.senate.gov/~lautenberg/

Rep. Jim Leach (IA)
http://www.house.gov/leach/

Sen. Patrick Leahy (VT)
http://www.senate.gov/~leahy/

Sen. Carl Levin (MI)
http://www.senate.gov/~levin/

Rep. John Lewis (GA)
http://www.house.gov/johnlewis/welcome.html

Sen. Joseph Lieberman (CT)
http://www.senate.gov/~lieberman/

Sen. Trent Lott (MS)
http://www.senate.gov/~lott/

Sen. Richard Lugar (IN)
http://www.senate.gov/~lugar/

M _____ M

Sen. Connie Mack (FL)
http://www.senate.gov/~mack/

Sen. John McCain (AZ)
http://www.senate.gov/~mccain/

Rep. Bill McCollum (FL)
http://www.house.gov/mccollum/

Sen. Mitch McConnell (KY)
http://www.senate.gov/~mcconnell/

If you find some dead links, please let us know at: http://www.celebritylocator.com/

Politics   Celebrity Web Site & E-Mail Directory

Rep. Cynyhia McKinney (GA)
http://www.house.gov/mckinney/

Sen. Barbara A. Mikulski (MD)
http://www.senate.gov/~mikulski/

Rep. Patsy T. Mink (HI)
http://www.house.gov/mink/

Sen. Daniel Patrick Moynihan (NY)
http://www.senate.gov/~moynihan/

Sen. Frank Murkowski (AK)
http://www.senate.gov/~murkowski/

Sen. Patty Murry (WA)
http://www.senate.gov/~murray/

N _____ N

Sen. Don Nickles (OK)
http://www.senate.gov/~nickles/

Rep. Eleanor Holmes Norton (DC)
http://www.house.gov/norton/

O _____ O

Sandra Day O'Connor
http://www2.lucidcafe.com/lucidcafe/library/96mar/oconnor.html

Rep. Solomon P. Ortiz (TX)
http://www.house.gov/ortiz/

P _____ P

Rep. Ron Packard (CA)
http://www.house.gov/packard/

If you find some dead links, please let us know at: http://www.celebritylocator.com/

Politics   Celebrity Web Site & E-Mail Directory

Governor George E. Pataki (NY)
http://www.state.ny.us/governor/

Rep. Donald Payne (NJ)
http://www.house.gov/payne/

Rep. Nancy Pelosi (CA)
http://www.house.gov/pelosi/

R   R

Rep. Charles B. Rangel (NY)
http://www.house.gov/rangel/

Justice William Rehnquist
http://www2.cybernex.net/~vanalst/william.html

Janet Reno
http://www.usdoj.gov/bios/jreno.html

Sen. Charles Robb (VA)
http://www.senate.gov/~robb/

Sen. John D. Rockefeller IV (WV)
http://www.senate.gov/~rockefeller/

Sec. Robert Rubin
http://www.ustreas.gov/

Gov. George H. Ryan (IL)
http://www.state.il.us/gov/

S   S

Justice Antonin Scalia
http://www2.cybernex.net/~vanalst/antonin.html

Sen. Charles Schumer (NY)
http://www.senate.gov/~schumer/

Sen. Richard Shelby (AL)
http://www.senate.gov/~shelby/

If you find some dead links, please let us know at: http://www.celebritylocator.com/

Politics Celebrity Web Site & E-Mail Directory

Sec. Rodney Slater
http://www.dot.gov/ost/

Sen. Olympia Snowe (ME)
http://www.senate.gov/~snowe/

Justice David Souter
http://www2.cybernex.net/~vanalst/david.html

Sen. Arlen Specter (PA)
http://www.senate.gov/~specter/

Sen. Ted Stevens (AK)
http://www.senate.gov/~stevens/

T   T

Gov. Bob Taft (OH)
http://www.ohio.gov/gov/

Justice Clarence Thomas
http://www2.cybernex.net/~vanalst/clarence.html

Sen. Fred Thompson (TN)
http://www.senate.gov/~thompson/

Gov. Tommy Thompson (WI)
http://www.wisgov.state.wi.us/

Sen. Strom Thurmond (SC)
http://www.senate.gov/~thurmond/

V   V

Rep. Nydia Velazques (NY)
http://www.house.gov/velazquez/

Gov. Jesse Ventura (MN)
http://www.governor.state.mn.us/

If you find some dead links, please let us know at: http://www.celebritylocator.com/

Politics   Celebrity Web Site & E-Mail Directory

Sen. George Voinovich (OH)
http://www.senate.gov/~voinovich/

W   W

Sen. John Warner (VA)
http://www.senate.gov/~warner/

Rep. Maxine Water (CA)
http://www.house.gov/waters/

Rep. J.C. Watts (OK)
http://www.house.gov/watts/

Rep. Henry Waxman (CA)
http://www.house.gov/waxman/

Sen. Paul Wellstone (MN)
http://www.senate.gov/~wellstone/

Sec. Tango West
http://www.va.gov/welcome.htm

Prince William
http://www.gilmer.net/royalty/

If you find some dead links, please let us know at: http://www.celebritylocator.com/

Others

To place an advertisement in this space,
call 734-761-4842 or E-mail:
axiominfo@celebritylocator.com

To place an advertisement in this space,
call 734-761-4842 or E-mail:
axiominfo@celebritylocator.com

To place an advertisement in this space,
call 734-761-4842 or E-mail:
axiominfo@celebritylocator.com

If you know a celebrity web site or
e-mail address that should be included
in this book, please e-mail it to us at:
axiominfo@celebritylocator.com

Others   Celebrity Web Site & E-Mail Directory

A

Dear Abby
http://www.uexpress.com/ups/abby/

Brandy Alexandre
http://www.kamikaze.org/

Angelie Almendare
http://www.angelie.com/

Carl Andrews, Jr.
http://www.maui.net/~carl/magic.html

Anagha
http://www.anagha.com/

Ant
http://www.artnet.net/~antcomicwb

Piers Anthony
http://www.hipiers.com/index.html

Roscoe "Fatty" Arbuckle
http://www.silent-movies.com/Arbucklemania/

Isaac Asimov
http://www.clark.net/pub/edseiler/WWW/asimov_home_page.html

B

Heywood Banks
http://www.heywoodbanks.com/

Tyra Banks
http://www.geocities.com/FashionAvenue/3062/PAGE15.HTML

Clive Barker
http://www.clivebarker.com/

If you find some dead links, please let us know at: http://www.celebritylocator.com/

Others Celebrity Web Site & E-Mail Directory

Tom Baxter
http://web.idirect.com/%7Etbhome/

Yasmine Bleeth
http://www.yasmine.net/

Judy Blume
http://www.judyblume.com/

Jan Burke
http://www.janburke.com/

C   C

James Cameron
http://www.angelfire.com/id/amazingcameron/

Naomi Campbell
http://web.tin.it/mirror/naomi/nc.html

Carrot Top
http://www.carrottop.com/

Agatha Christie
http://www.hi.is/~ragnaj/

Arthur C. Clark
http://www.lsi.usp.br/~rbianchi/clarke/

Michael Collins
http://www.michaelcollins.com/

Billy Connolly
http://www.sarsen.demon.co.uk/billy/billy.html

David Copperfield
http://www.dcopperfield.com/

Douglas Coupland
http://www.coupland.com/

If you find some dead links, please let us know at: http://www.celebritylocator.com/

Others   Celebrity Web Site & E-Mail Directory

Cindy Crawford
http://www.cindy.com/

D   D

Diana, Princess of Whales
http://www.groupweb.com/personal/lstyle/diana_memory.htm

Salvador Dali
http://wildsau.idv.uni-linz.ac.at/~chris/Dali/

E   E

Amelia Earhart
http://www.ionet.net:80/~jellenc/ae_intro.html

Nichole Eggert
http://www.prism.gatech.edu/~gt4391b/nichole.html

Albert Einstein
http://www.westegg.com/einstein/

Emme
http://www.emmesupermodel.com/

Angie Everhart
http://www.geocities.com/Hollywood/Set/1345/

F   F

Fabio
http://www.northcoast.com/~shojo/Fabio/fabio.html

The Family Jewels
http://www.tfj.com/tfj/

Al Fike
http://www.alfike.com/

If you find some dead links, please let us know at: http://www.celebritylocator.com/

Others   Celebrity Web Site & E-Mail Directory

Ken Follett
http://www.ken-follett.com/

Glen Foster
http://www.glenfoster.com/

G   G

Gallagher
http://www.gallaghersmash.com/

Bill Gates
http://www.microsoft.com/BillGates/

Yasmeen Ghauri
http://www.td-sanchez.com/yasmeen/index.shtml

Martha Grimes
http://www.marthagrimes.com/

H   H

Prof. Stephen Hawkins
http://www.psyclops.com/hawking/

Eva Herzigova
http://www.iwcdesign.com/eva/

Alfred Hitchcock
http://www.primenet.com/~mwc/

Harry Houdini
http://www.uelectric.com/houdini/houdini.html

Rachel Hunter
http://www.scar.utoronto.ca/~96chungs/rachel.htm

If you find some dead links, please let us know at: http://www.celebritylocator.com/

Others Celebrity Web Site & E-Mail Directory

I

Kathy Ireland
http://www.kathyireland.com/

J

The Jerkyboys
http://www.thejerkyboys.com/

Pope John Paul II
http://www.zpub.com/un/pope/

Erica Jong
http://www.ericajong.com/

Tom Joyner
http://www.tjms.com

K

Dr. Jack Kevorkian
http://www.rights.org/~deathnet/KevorkianFile.html

Stephen King
http://www.stephenking.com/

Barbara Kingsolver
http://www.kingsolver.com/

L

Bob Larson
http://www.cris.com/~Ranger57/blm.shtml

Timothy Leary
http://leary.com/

Rush Limbaugh
http://www.rtis.com/nat/pol/rush/

If you find some dead links, please let us know at: http://www.celebritylocator.com/

Others   Celebrity Web Site & E-Mail Directory

David Lynch
http://www.mikedunn.com/lynch/

M   M

Elle MacPherson
http://www.microsaft.com/elle/

Cindy Margolis
http://www.cindymargolis.com/

Valeria Mazza
http://www.valeria.com.ar/

James A. Michener
http://www.jamesmichener.com/

Chris Moore
http://www.chrismoore.com/

Toni Morrison
http://www.luminarium.org/contemporary/tonimorrison/

Kate Moss
http://www.angelfire.com/ct/LoveLeo/index.html

N   N

Cori Nadine
http://www.corinadine.com/

Nico
http://www.netpoint.be/abc/nico/

P   P

Bettie Page
http://www.grrl.com/betty.html

Vanessa Paradis
http://welcome.to/vanessa.paradis/

If you find some dead links, please let us know at: http://www.celebritylocator.com/

Others   Celebrity Web Site & E-Mail Directory

Penn & Teller
http://www.sincity.com/

Daniela Pestova
http://members.xoom.com/Shylocks/Daniela.htm

Emo Philips
http://www.nd.edu/%7Eemerkler/emo/emo.html

Edgar Allan Poe
http://www.comnet.ca/~forrest/

Maury Povich
http://gladstone.uoregon.edu/~wbeutler/maury.htm

Chef Paul Prudhomme
http://www.chefpaul.com/table.html

R   R

Anne Rice
http://www.annerice.com/

Douglas Rushkoff
http://www.levity.com/rushkoff/index.html

S   S

Dr. Laura Schlessinger
http://www.drlaura.com/frames.html

Claudia Schiffer
http://www.glassrose.com/

Siegfried & Roy
http://www.sarmoti.com/index.html

Richard Simmons
http://www.richardsimmons.com/

If you find some dead links, please let us know at: http://www.celebritylocator.com/

Others   Celebrity Web Site & E-Mail Directory

Peter Sosna
http://pw1.netcom.com/~psosna/magic.html

Daniell Steel
http://www.daniellesteel.com/

Howard Stern
http://www.sternradio.com/

Oliver Stone
http://www.geocities.com/Hollywood/2682/

T   T

Quentin Tarantino
http://members.xoom.com/Tarantino/

Scott Thompson
http://www.scottland.com/scott.htm

Christy Turlington
http://www.djuna.simplenet.com/christy/index.html

V   V

Frederique Van der Wal
http://www.supermodel.com/featured/fred/index.html

Dr. Jack Van Impe
http://www.jvim.com/

Vendela
http://www.light-saber.com/vk/

W   W

Andy Warhol
http://imv.aau.dk/~jfogde/biografi.html

If you find some dead links, please let us know at: http://www.celebritylocator.com/

Others   Celebrity Web Site & E-Mail Directory

Dr. Bill Wattenburg
http://www.pushback.com/Wattenburg/

William Wegman
http://www.wegmanworld.com/

Tom Wolfe
http://www.tomwolfe.com/

If you find some dead links, please let us know at: http://www.celebritylocator.com/

E-mail Addresses

To place an advertisement in this space,
call 734-761-4842 or E-mail:
axiominfo@celebritylocator.com

To place an advertisement in this space,
call 734-761-4842 or E-mail:
axiominfo@celebritylocator.com

To place an advertisement in this space,
call 734-761-4842 or E-mail:
axiominfo@celebritylocator.com

If you know a celebrity web site or
e-mail address that should be included
in this book, please e-mail it to us at:
axiominfo@celebritylocator.com

E-Mail Addresses Celebrity Web Site & E-Mail Directory

-A-
Scott Adams
scottadams@aol.com

Daniel Adlerman
Bookkids@aol.com

Kim Adlerman
kimarts@aol.com

Aerosmith
vindaloo@hooked.net

Agape
sabbi@limestone.kosone.com

Marilyn Agee
mjagee@kiwi.net

Alice in Chains
AICFC@speakeasy.org

Tim Allen
tim@morepower.com

Allman Brothers
rowlanda@allmanbrothersband.com

Angelie Almendare
mail@angelie.com

Amy Alpine
amyalpine@aol.com

Rosalyn Alsobrook
r.alsobrook@genie.geis.com

Amazing Randi
76702.3507@compuserve.com

Kevin J. Anderson
kevreb@aol.com

Pamela Anderson-Lee
pambonell@aol.com

Paul Anka
ANKAPA@aol.com

Jennifer Anniston
jeffr48196@aol.com

Piers Anthony
hi-piers@ix.netcom.com

Jane Asher
info@jane-asher.co.uk

Kaitlyn Ashley
monty17@msn.com

Ed Asner
72726.357@compuserve.com

Asphalt Canyon
noodle@sirius.com

Audio Adrenaline
bobaa@aol.com

Medeleine Albright
secretary@state.gov

-B-
Bruce Babbitt
bruce_babbitt@ios.doi.gov

Baby Alive
xemu@xemu.com

Bad Boy Entertainment
bad.boy@bmge.com

Oksana Baiul
fnemporium@aol.com

If you find some incorrect addresses, please let us know at: http://www.celebritylocator.com/

E-Mail Addresses   Celebrity Web Site & E-Mail Directory

Melissa Baldwin
lissabee@cts.com

Tyra Banks
lucy56@aol.com

Bob Barker
price@www.cbs.com

John Perry Barlow
barlow@eff.org

Nevada Barr
NevadaBarr@compuserve.com

Paul Bearer
WWFBearer@aol.com

Pat Benatar
cowgirl@pacificnet.net

Darren Bennett
nflaussie@aol.com

Nigel Bennett
NBenn81369@aol.com

Sen. Joseph A. Biden
senator@biden.senate.gov

Craig Biggo
hof2ndbaseman@hotmail.com

Scott Blackwell
NSoul@aol.com

Bone Thugs N Harmony
Leathafase@aol.com

J.R. Bookwalter
tempe@earthlink.net

Gillian Bonner
webmistress@blackdragon.com

Boston
bandmail@Boston.org

George Boyce
glenara@aol.com

David Boyd
dboyd@eworld.com

Sen. Barbara Boxer
Senator@Boxer.senate.gov

Bozo The Clown
BOZO@tribune.com

Pat Brady
PBradyRose@aol.com

Sen. John Breaux
senator@breaux.senate.gov

David Brenner
hibrenner@aol.com

Tom Brokaw
nightly@nbc.com

Dr. Bill Bright
elvin@mdalink.com

Alan Brimm
bfa@slip.net

James L. Brooks
72700.2062@compuserve.com

Brooks & Dunn
BrooksDunn@brooks-dunn.com

If you find some incorrect addresses, please let us know at: http://www.celebritylocator.com/

E-Mail Addresses Celebrity Web Site & E-Mail Directory

Rep. George Brown
talk2geb@mail.house.gov

Jerry Brown
75300.3105@compuserve

Sen. Richard Bryan
senator@bryan.senate.gov.

Zachery Bryan
zachery@morepower.com

Pat Buchanan
76326.126@compuserve.com

Mike Burger
mikeb@homeandfamily.com

Jan Burke
jan@janburke.com

CH Burnett
chburn@execpc.com

Sen. Conrad Burns
conrad_burns@burns.senate.gov

Gov Jeb Bush
fl_governor@eog.state.fl.us

Robert Byrd
senator_byrd@byrd.senate.gov

-C-
Nicholas Cage
niccage@hotmail.com

Bruce Campbell
bcautographs@bccentral.com

Drew Carey
DrewsCShow@aol.com

Gov. Paul Cellucci
GOffice@state.ma.us

Center of Attention
mbros@sils.umich.edu

Vinton Cerf
vcerf@CNRI.va.us

Sen. John Chafee
senator_chafee@chafee.senate.gov

Jackie Chan
jackie@jackiechan.com

Charo
fanclub@charo.com

The Choir
choirline@aol.com

Tom Clancy
tomclancy@aol.com

Terry Ike Clanton
clanton1@ix.netcom.com

Blake Clark
Blakeman22@aol.com

Roger Clemens
roger.clemens@bluejays.ca

Prsident Bill Clinton
President@whitehouse.gov

Hillary Rodham-Clinton
First.Lady@whitehouse.gov

Kristen Cloke
kcloke@servtech.com

If you find some incorrect addresses, please let us know at: http://www.celebritylocator.com/

E-Mail Addresses   Celebrity Web Site & E-Mail Directory

George Clooney
g_clooney@nbs.er.com

Coal Chamber
coalchamber@mysti.com

Kristi Coasts
wdz@ix.netcom.com

Sen. Thad Cochran
senator@cochran.senate.gov

Allan Cole
75130.2761@compuserve.com

Steve Coleman
mbase@epix.net

Jamie Owens Collins
dwc@earthlink

Judy Collins
rmprod@aol.com

Sean "Puffy" Combs
PuffyDad35@aol.com

Coolio
coolio@gangster.com

Tommy Coomes
coomesie@aol.com

Sen. Kent Conrad
HomePage@conrad.senate.gov

Continuim
danb@baronet.demon.co.uk

Rep. John Conyers
John.Conyers@mail.house.gov

Lydia Cornell
LYDIAC000@aol.com

Country Gamblers Band
lwarren@adsnet.com

Yvonne Craig
batgirl@yvonnecraig.com

The Cranberries
fnemporium@aol.com

Quentin Crisp
HRHQCrisp@aol.com

Jason Cropper
jchoplllll@aol.com

Sheryl Crow
sherylcrow@thelot.com

Crowdies House
jraymond2@compuserve.com

The Cure
thecure@thecure.com

Adam Curry
adam@metaverse.com

-D-
Mark Dacascos
dacascos-mail@weblore.com

Dakoda Motor Co.
mbisonl@aol.com

Timothy Dalton
GSFE@aol.com

Rodney Dangerfield
rodney@rodney.com

If you find some incorrect addresses, please let us know at: http://www.celebritylocator.com/

E-Mail Addresses   Celebrity Web Site & E-Mail Directory

Linda Dano
LindaDano@nashville.com

Sen. Tom Daschle
tom_daschle@daschle.senate.gov

Dave Matthews Band
dmband@redlt.com

Greg Davis
duffers@halcyon.com

Dead Family
ari@deadfamily.com

Dead Man's Curve
deadman@jukebox.demon.co.uk

Calvert DeForest
:calvert@calvertdeforest.com

Sen. Mike DeWine
webmaster@dewine.senate.gov

Diamond Rio
driofanclub@juno.com

Dick Dietrick
nitestnd@aol.com

Sen. Christopher Dobb
senator@dodd.senate.gov

Sen. Pete Domenici
Senator_Domenici@Domenici.Senate.Gov

The Doors
info@thedoors.com

Debbe Dunning
debbe@morepower.com

-E-
Roger Ebert
73136.3232@compuserve.com

Clint Eastwood
rowdiyates@aol.com

Greg Evans
geluann@aol.com

-F-
Kevin Fagan
kevinfagan@aol.com

Faze Productions
Faze_Productions@eriss.com

Sen. Dianne Feinstein
senator@feinstein.senate.gov

Giselle Fernande
gfernandez@nbc.com

Ferron
ferronfan@FerronWeb.com

Paul Fieg
heyhiboy@aol.com

Al Fike
alfike@usa.net

First Church of Chumbawamba
feedback@chumba.com

John Fischer
JWFisher@aol.com

Raymond Floyd
rayfloyd@rayfloyd.com

If you find some incorrect addresses, please let us know at: http://www.celebritylocator.com/

E-Mail Addresses   Celebrity Web Site & E-Mail Directory

Focus
jmfocus@aol.com

Ross Forman
ROSSWCW@aol.com

Vivica Fox
vivica@vivicafox.com

Fournier Francine
FrancineECW@webtv.net

Robert Fulghum
70771.763@compuserve.com

-G-
William "Bill" Gates
billg@microsoft.com

Jennifer Gatti
gatti@n2.net

Mac Gayden
gayden1@boone.net

Rep. Richard Gephardt
gephardt@mail.house.gov

Mel Gibson
mel_gibson@hotmail.com

Chuck Girard
chuck@chuck.org

Seth Godin
sgp@sgp.com

Vice-President Al Gore
vice.president@whitehouse.gov

Sen. Bob Graham (FL)
bob_graham@graham.senate.gov

Amy Grant
amy.grant@nashville.com

Jack Graue
oopinmoo@msn.com

The Greaseman
GreaseShow@aol.com

Ken Griffey, Jr.
Keng@mariners.com

Martha Grimes
grimesinfo@plesser.com

The Gumbi Band
theband@thegumbiband.com

-H-
Senator Chuck Hagel
chuck_hagel@hagel.senate.gov

Hanson Brothers
hansonfans@hansonline.com

Senator Tom Harkin
tom_harkin@harkin.senate.gov

Senator Orrin Hatch
senator_hatch@Hatch.senate.gov

Isaac Hayes
IHProductions@banet.net

Brenda Henson
sisterspir@aol.com

Wanda Henson
sisterspir@aol.com

Faith Hill
faithfan@thebook.com

If you find some incorrect addresses, please let us know at: http://www.celebritylocator.com/

E-Mail Addresses   Celebrity Web Site & E-Mail Directory

Earl Hindman
earl@morepower.com

Don Ho
dhoel@lava.net

Xaviera Hollander
Xaviera@xs4all.nl

Nancy Honeytree
jr@onehundred.com

Bob Hope
Bobhope@bobhope.com

Sir Anthony Hopkins
sirhopkins@aol.com

Larry Howard
LHBluesman@aol.com

Lisa Howard
earth@roddenberry.com

Brit Hume
72737.357@compuerserve.com

Sean Hurley
smhurley@micron.net

Olivia Hussey
frzflame24@earthlink.net

Rep. Asa Hutchinson
Asa.Hutchinson@mail.house.gov

Sen. Kay Bailey Hutchison
senator@hutchison.senate.gov

-I-
Initial Charge Band
xemu@xemu.com

Insane Clown Posse
JellyNuts@insaneclownposse.com

-J-
Jack Mack & The Heart Attack
jpbp@aol.com

Jana Jae
janajae.com

Jamiroquai
webmaster@jamiroquai.co.uk

Mike Jansen
Skyward@cris.com

Helen Jayne
helenjayne@msn.com

Senator Jim Jeffords
vermont@jeffords.senate.gov

Grant R. Jeffrey
grantr.jeffrey@sympatico.ca

Jewel
Jeweljk@aol.com

Don Johnson
katejones1@aol.com

Jimmy Johnson (cartoonist)
arlnjan@aol.com

Senator Tim Johnson
tim@johnson.senate.gov

Erica Jong
jongleur@pipeline.com

Wynonna Judd
wifc@nashville.net

If you find some incorrect addresses, please let us know at: http://www.celebritylocator.com/

E-Mail Addresses   Celebrity Web Site & E-Mail Directory

-K-
Karl Pabst & the Blue Ribbon
kdpbluribn@aol.com

Casey Kasem
Casey4300@aol.com

Ronan Keating
ronan@hg4.com

Garrison Keillor
gkeillor@madmax.mpr.org

Dr. D. James Kennedy
djk@cr-online.com

Senator Ted Kennedy
senator@kennedy.senate.gov

Senator John Kerry
john_kerry@kerry.senate.gov

Marianne Kesler
coolspirit@juno.com

Alan Keys
70744.1235@compuserve.com

Rabih EL-Khawli
rkawli@echo-on.net

Michael E. Knight
CBMouser@aol.com

Wayne Knight
71054.2032@compuserve.com

KRUSH
davem@fia.net

Senator Jon Kyl
info@kyl.senate.gov

-L-
Ricki Lake
rickilake@aol.com

Senator Mary Landrieu
senator@landrieu.senate.gov

Danni Leigh
info@dannileigh.com

David Letterman
lateshow@pipeline.com

Senator Carl Levin
senator@levin.senate.gov

G. Gordon Liddy
potent357@aol.com

Rush Limbaugh
70277.2502@compuserve.com

Rick London
force@c-gate.net

Sen. Trent Lott
senatorlott@lott.senate.gov

Courtney Love
lilacs00@aol.com

Mark Lowry
marklowry@marklowry.com

Lucias Tokas Band
'marto8@seacoast.com

-M-
Madonna
Madonna@wbr.com

Bill Maher
pi@cis.compuserve.com

If you find some incorrect addresses, please let us know at: http://www.celebritylocator.com/

E-Mail Addresses   Celebrity Web Site & E-Mail Directory

Mary Maitlin
marymcbs@cais.com

Manic Street Preachers
manics@manics.co.uk

Dr. Geoffrey March
gmarch@stars.sfsu.edu

Cindy Margolis
cindcen@aol.com

Kitty Margolis
kittym@kittymargolis.com

Marky Mark
marky@kalifornia.com

Pamela Sue Martin
pamsuemart@aol.com

Dana Mase
dana@danamase.com

MasterP
schmid@masterp.org

Dave Matthews Band
fanmail@dmband.com

Dawson McAllister
dmlive@christianradio.com

Sen. John McCain
John_McCain@McCain.senate.gov

Jenny McCarthy
jmccarthy@mailcity.com

Kimberly M'Carver
kimber@flash.net

Rep. Bill McCollum
bill.mccollum@mail.house.gov

Senator Mitch McConnell
senator@mcconnell.senate.gov

Maureen McCormick
mccormick@ttinet.com

Julie McCullough
JulieMcCul@aol.com

Bobby McFerrin
info@bobbymcferrin.com

Roger McGuinn
rmcguinn@ix.netcom.com

William McNamara
mcnamara@servtech.com

Jim Meddick
JimMeddick@aol.com

Leslie Meek
leslie@smartnet.net

Sen. Daniel P. Moynihan
Senator@dpm.senate.gov

Sen. Frank Murkowski
email@murkowski.senate.gov

Sen. Patsy Murray
senator_murray@murray.senate.gov

N
Sen. Don Nickles
senator@nickles.senate.gov

If you find some incorrect addresses, please let us know at: http://www.celebritylocator.com/

E-Mail Addresses   Celebrity Web Site & E-Mail Directory

P
Melon Patch
melonheads@aol.com

Men out Loud
menoutloud@earthlink.net

Metallica
metclub@aol.com

Alyssa Milano
angell@primenet.com

Mista Tru
Mista_tru@juno.com

Moby Grape
MobyGrape@Geocities.com

Katy Moffatt
kmwhq@mcleodusa.net

Eddie Money
EDDIEMNY@aol.com

T.S. Monk
tsmonk@jazzcorner.com

John Michael Montgomery
jmm@johnmichael.com

Demi Moore
Demim2aol.com

Glen Morgan
Gam5@aol.com

Toni Morrison
morrison@princeton.edu

Bob Mortimer
bobmortimer@hotmail.com

Kate Mulgrew
kmulgrew@rocketmail.com

-N-
Kevin Naylor
knaylor@digitalexp

David Nelson Band
dnb@nelsonband.com

Gunnar Nelson
GunNelson@aol.com

Matthew Nelson
MatNelson@aol.com

Stevie Nick
stevie@fanmailink.com

Anna Nicole
live@annalive.com

Mike Nesmith
nez@primenet.com

Ted Nugent
75162.2032@compuserve.com

Bill Nye
billnye@nyelabs.com

-O-
Oak Ridge Boys
jon@oakridgeboys.com

Oasis
oasis@oasisinet.com

Conan O'Brien
latenight@nbc.com

If you find some incorrect addresses, please let us know at: http://www.celebritylocator.com/

E-Mail Addresses   Celebrity Web Site & E-Mail Directory

Miles O'Brien
70230.2064@compuserve.com

Renee O'Connor
RocMailer@aol.com

Rosie O'Donnell
(contact at website below)
http://rosieo.warnerbros.com/cmp/contact.htm

Edward James Olmos
lmh@kepplerassociates.com

Ashley Olsen
MKAFunClub@aol.com

Mary Kate Olsen
MKAFunClub@aol.com

Once Hush
oncehush@finetune.co

Yoko Ono
Yoko@yoko.com

Ozzy Osbourne
WORLDOFOZZ@aol.com

Rick Overton
72162.1701@compuserve.com

-P-
Julie Parrish
JParr18031@aol.com

Gram Parsons
larryk@customeraccess.com

Gov. George Pataki
gov.pataki@chamber.state.ny.us

Jillette Penn
penn@delphi.com

Ross Perot
71511.460@compuserve.com

John Perry
barlow@eff.org

Pessimist Black Death Metal
pess666@ix.netcom.com

Mike Peters
grimmy@gate.net

Petra
petra@wordrecords.com

Phish
info@phish.net

Lincoln Pierce
drawnate@aol.com

Mandie Pinto
pntobmr@aol.com

Brad Pitt
rodrigocotasauce@hotmail.com

Jean-Luc ponty
jean-luc@ponty.com

Paula Poundstone
paula@mojones.com

Stefanie Powers
stefanie@fansource.com

Hillary Price
hprice@aol.com

Pat Priest
priest000@aol.com

If you find some incorrect addresses, please let us know at: http://www.celebritylocator.com/

E-Mail Addresses   Celebrity Web Site & E-Mail Directory

Primus
bobcock@primussucks.com

Chef Paul Prudhomme
info@chefpaul.com

-R-
Keanu Reeves
reeves23@aol.com

Burt Reynolds
smokeymail@aol.com

Patricia Richardson
patricia@aol.com

Don Rickles
dj@hifrontier.com

Leann Rimes
larfans@leann.com

Geraldo Rivera
GeraldoCBS@aol.com

Sen. Charles S. Robb
senator@robb.senate.gov

David Robinson
Noelh@theadmiral.com

Sen. John Rockefeller
senator@rockefeller.senate.gov

Majel Roddenberry
stinfo@roddenberry.com

Dennis Rodman
worm@rodman.org

Al Roker
Mailbag@roker.com

Ann Rule
annier37@aol.com

Buddy Ryan
BuddyRyan@aol.com

Jeri Lynn Ryan
scimedjo@dhc.net

-S-
Buffy Saint-Marie
bsm@aloha.net

Summer Sanders
SummerSanders@medalists.com

Adam Sandler
sandler@cris.com

Marie Sansone
RiaABC@aol.com

Devon Sawa
dsawa@pacificcoast.net

John Schneider
JRSFWPS@aol.com

Sen. Richard Shelby
senator@shelby.senate.gov

Kenny Shepherd
KWSband@aol.com

Grant Show
grant-show@fan.net

Silverchair
mail@chairpage.com

Tucker Smallwood
Tuck914@aol.com

If you find some incorrect addresses, please let us know at: http://www.celebritylocator.com/

E-Mail Addresses Celebrity Web Site & E-Mail Directory

Amber Smith
ambersite@webtv.net-

Beau Smith
BeauSmith@aol.com

Ozzie Smith
ozzies@ozziesmith.com

Taran Noah Smith
taran@morepower.com

Wesley Snipes
herukush@aol.com

Tom Snyder
latelateshow@cbs.com

Soundgarden
sgfc@speakeasy.org

Britney Spears
britney@peeps.com

Sen. Arlen Specter
Senator_Specter@Specter.senate

Robin Spielberg
spobs@access.digex.net

Squirrel Nut Zippers
snz@mindspring.com

Tim Stack
nightstand@segi-mail.com

Lisa Stahl
LisaStahl1@aol.com

Scott Stantis
thebuckets@aol.com

Danielle Steele
awsomed@aol.com

Steely Dan
STEELYDAN@STEELYDAN.COM

Jim Steinman
steinman@1webplaza.com

Howard Stern
stern@urshan.com

Ray Stevens
rstevens@raystevens.com

Sen. Ted Stevens
senator_stevens@stevens.senate.gov

Crystal Storm
seestorm@aol.com

John Stossel
stossel@abc.com

George Strait
fanclub@georgestraitfans.com

Rider Strong
letters@riderstrong.com

Superdrag
SDRAG7@aol.com

Andy Summers
info@andysummers.com

-T-
Ty Tabor
76702.3455@compuserve.com

Stacy Taylor
Stacytylr@aol.com

If you find some incorrect addresses, please let us know at: http://www.celebritylocator.com/

E-Mail Addresses   Celebrity Web Site & E-Mail Directory

Tenison Twins
twins@tenisontwins.com

Keith Thibedeaux
earth.people@juno.com

Allyson Thomas
allysin@hotmail.com

Jonathan Taylor Thomas
jonathan@morepower.com

Sen. Fred Thompson
senator_thompson@thompson.senate.gov

Gov. Tommy Thompson
wisgov@mail.state.wi.us

Tool
toolband@well.net

Hunter Tylo
CJNA67C@prodigy.com

Tricky
aboo@primenet.com

-U-
Under The Bridge
kdc@bbs.gaianet.net.

Robert Urich
robert@roberturich.com

-V-
Steve Vaile
gemstone@teleport.com

Dr. Jack Van Impe
jvimi@vim.com

Greg Vaughn
GREGV000@aol.com

Gov. Jesse Ventura
jesse.ventura@state.mn.us

Asia Vieira
Asia558543@aol.com

Vigilantes of Love
VOLMail@aol.com

Violent Femmes
dv@vfemmes.com

Vitamin F
vitamin@aol.com

Voice of Purity
ca_cameron@yumaeld.k12.az.us

Jenna Von oy
pedrew@aol.com

-W-
Bob Wall
Walltime@aol.com

Joe Walsh
raycraft@post.avnet.co.uk

Matthew Ward
mward@e-tex.com

Dick Warlock
DickWarlock@hotmail.com

Sen. John Warner
senator@warner.senate.gov

Rep. J.C. Watts
rep.jcwatts@mail.house.gov

Andrew Lloyd Webber
rucny@reallyuseful.com

If you find some incorrect addresses, please let us know at: http://www.celebritylocator.com/

E-Mail Addresses   Celebrity Web Site & E-Mail Directory

Bill Welch
Bill.Welch@pressroom.com

Adam West
AdamBatman@aol.com

Bob West
bobwest1@aol.com

Byran White
ByranOK@aol.com

White Heart
WhiteHeart@curb.com

Christine Todd Whitman
cwhitman@rutgers.edu

Van Williams
VanWilliam@aol.com

Oprah Winfrey
harpo@interaccess.com

Steve Winwood
fanmail@stevewinwood.com

Annie Wood
bzzzshow@aol.com

James Woods
jameswoods@aol.com

Louise Woodward
support@louise.force9.co.uk

Chely Wright
webmaster@chely.com

Noah Wyle
noahwer@aol.com

-X
Xuxa
xuxa@ibm.net

Y
Trisha Yearwood
webmaster@totallytrisha.com

Young Dubliners
dubs@youngdubs.com

-Z-
Laurie Z
ZLAURIE@aol.com

If you find some incorrect addresses, please let us know at: http://www.celebritylocator.com/

MAKE CONTACT WITH THE STARS!

The Celebrity Directory™ 2000-2001 covers the entire spectrum of celebrities. If a person is famous or worth locating, it's almost certain that their address can be found in here.
ISBN 0-943213-35-5
Only $39.95+$3.95 postage & handling

The 2000-2001 Star Guide™ is the most reliable and up-to-date guide available for over 3200 addresses of major stars from every field.
ISBN 0-943213-34-7
Only $14.95+$3.00 postage & handling

The Celebrity Birthday Guide™ (4th Edition) lists the birthdays of celebrities past and present. Thousands of entries by calendar date.
ISBN 0-943213-25-8
Only $10.95+$3.00 postage & handling

The 2000-2001 Celebrity Website and E-mail Directory™ is the most reliable and up-to-date guide available for thousands of web sites and e-mail addresses of major celebrities from every field.
ISBN 0-943213-33-9
Only $9.95 + $3.00 postage and handling

Use the **Celebrity Birthday Directory™ (4th Edition)** to find the birthdays of your favorite celebrities. Alphabetized for quick reference.
ISBN 0-943213-26-6
Only $10.95+$3.00 postage & handling

The Celebrity Locator 2000-2001™ is the ultimate guide for locating celebrities. If a person is famous and worth locating, chances are you'll find their snail mail, e-mail, fan club, and website address in here.
ISBN 0-943213-32-0
Only $79.95 + $3.95 postage & handling.

Mail completed form to:
AXIOM INFORMATION RESOURCES • P.O. Box 8015-T8 • Ann Arbor, MI 48107 • USA

Name_____

Address_____

City_____ State_____ Zip_____

_____ Copies of **Celebrity Directory**™ @ $39.95 each + $3.95 P&H
_____ Copies of **Star Guide**™ @ $14.95 each + $3.00 P&H
_____ Copies of **Celebrity Birthday Guide**™ @ $10.95 each + $3.00 P&H
_____ Copies of **Celebrity E-mail&Website Directory**™ @ $9.95 each + $3.00 P&H
_____ Copies of **Celebrity Birthday Directory**™ @ $10.95 each + $3.00 P&H
_____ Copies of **Celebrity Locator**™ @ $79.95 each + $3.95 P&H

Total Order $_____,_____

(Add $3.20 per item for 2nd DAY PRIORITY MAIL)➤ Total Postage & Handling $_____,_____

*Michigan Sales Tax:
Celebrity Directory-$2.40 • Star Guide-78¢ • Celebrity Birthday Guide-66¢ • Celebrity E-mail & Website Guide-60¢ • Celebrity Birthday Directory-66¢ • Celebrity Locator-$4.80

MI Residents add 6% Sales Tax * $_____,_____

Total Enclosed $_____,_____